2012 Cover....

REVISION: Summer, 2018.

In this book you are now reading, (cover above) - I invited 'significant friends' to share their perspectives on the principles outlined in the book. I have written this revision to do some things personal & relevant to me regarding the content. Essentially I wanted to do some serious 'rambling' in hitting on a lot of pieces & bits I wanted to share with you. Enjoy!

Doug

SIGNIFICANCE
Starts Now

...How We Live Our Lives Matters!

Author:

Doug Booker

(Revised Summer 2018)

Significance Starts Now 2012 © Doug Booker.
All rights strictly reserved by Doug Booker and
Booker Training Associates.

First Printing: 2012
ISBN: 978-0615727738

Printed in the USA

Publishing/Editorial Assistance: Derek Kenner

"...give credit to others!", etc:

I stress this (above) principle in my teaching and work with leaders. I will therefore practice what I preach and give credit to God for all I am, all I have learned, and all I have to share here.

I must also give credit to my parents/family; the great people in the little town where I was raised (Lexington, Missouri) and the myriad of friends, teachers, coaches, mentors and leaders I have learned with through all seasons of life.

FYI: Throughout this read - I am using quotes, images, pictures, phrases, and thoughts which I have picked up during life – and no doubt, concepts internalized from others. I have given credit when/where I know from which they came. For everything else used within, I say THANKS anonymously for them being placed in my path. Little is new in this world; what I share here is some of what I have learned, and digested.

I believe the content and intent of this book to be Godly and biblically-based and worldly-accepted as truth and best practices for one and ALL of us. However it is not presented here to press my faith on you; I promise.

****

*I have intentionally provided space throughout for 'your thoughts' - along with some blank pages at the very end. This book was intended to make you think...and capture your thoughts in writing.

For eBook & Kindle Readers, I strongly urge you to have some paper/pencil ready at hand.

DEDICATION

To Danny Schneider  August 26, 1943 - July 6, 2012

During the writing of this work, Danny left us for a much more significant place, away from this world as we know it. I am sure he is in a better place and am happy for that. It was one of those good things many might say, in our losing Danny from this earth. That is always so strange and awkward to say, but likely true. All who knew him surely miss him and his significance!

Danny lived a life exemplified by love, kindness, service and the forgiveness of others. Danny had a life filled with abundant quality relationships in every direction. The principles within this book were exemplified by him and who he *was* in his walk.

Danny came into my life when my sister fell in love and married him over 20 years ago. I was hesitant initially, thinking he wasn't good enough for *my* sister. It turns out I was very wrong. He was a significant person who lived a life that blessed all who entered his path. He made a difference in my life and many others whose presence he blessed ...of this I am positive.

✶✶✶

Danny's wife, Phyllis Schneider deserves mention here as well. His wife and my sister clearly walk these principles in life. The courage, love, commitment and support she gives people in general and gave Danny always (especially *in his final season)* is truly significant.

I must also say thanks to my parents for the environment of love and being wonderful teachers, leaders and models in my life. So much I know and so much I am is because of them.

TABLE OF CONTENTS

PREFACE	p.	8
INTRO (PERSPECTIVES)	p.	9
<u>PRINCIPLES</u>	p.	48
PEACE	p.	52
FORGIVENESS	p.	72
SERVICE	p.	83
LEARNER	p.	96
TRANSPARENCY	p.	131
THANKFULNESS	p.	147
LOVE / RELATIONSHIP	p.	157
FRUITFULNESS	p.	181
WRAP UP / CONCLUSION	p.	193
PIECES OF SIGNIFICANCE	p.	207
SELF-ASSESSMENT	p.	223
EPITAPH / MISSION	p.	228
AUTHOR	p.	231

PREFACE

Doug's book on 'Significance' is an inspirational and groundbreaking work on the reality of viewing our lives, and others around us, as—significant. Doug creates a thought provoking journey for us as he explores the basic principles of what significance means and how we might use it in our lives. As we join him on this journey we are able to explore the definitions of significance, how they apply to our lives, how we might increase the level of significance in our lives, and most importantly, how we might help others do the same.

One of the vital contributions of this book is the focus on how you and I, as individuals, might understand and use our personal significance as fundamental life characteristics that— if we use them to the highest possible degree— will improve, change, and enhance the lives of others with whom we come in contact.

Doug's life experiences prove to be a sound and solid foundation for identifying and exploring —SIGNIFICANCE in many practical ways. It is a book based on Doug's 30 years of serving as a —leader of leaders & a teacher of leadership. He uses these experiences as a backdrop showing us how we might grow in —significance. In ourselves and others.

As a teacher, Doug has called upon the many teaching and learning situations he has witnessed and gives us, the reader, the benefit of countless and multifaceted examples of —significance‖ in the lives of his students. As a man of faith, Doug shares with us how his faith serve as a very practical and strong foundation for exploring and believing in the idea of leading a —significant life.

Significance Starts Now is where you should begin to develop a stronger understanding of what significance is and how it might best be applied in our society. The book is a solid read that helps us learn how we might start the beginning of living truly significant lives- beginning now.

Dr. Derek Kenner

INTRODUCTION

Some of the most prolific books written have been about philosophy and our purpose in life. Sooner or later, I am convinced everyone wants or desires to discover clarity of purpose. At some point we all seek significance both in our lives and what we do. I have heard it said that (they) say:

'WITHOUT PURPOSE, WE WITHER & DIE'

I believe this statement more and more and more as I age; as I experience life and observe people in my life.

This writing is about 'significance' - in the approach we take in moving toward our purpose; it is about the journey.

It is said that wisdom comes with age and experience. As we all age, we all likely begin to understand and agree with that statement. Not that I'm 'aged' yet, but I am indeed beginning to feel the essence of this thought.

My hope is that this book can and will lead to some even younger than me; cause some youth to 'realize some HOW to(s)' regarding how to lead lives of significance, substance and even worldly success. For those already seasoned, my prayer is that the content will increase your significance as well. Or at least receive your blessings as truth!

Wherever you are in life, it is not too late to become significant as we were all purposed to be. I believe that to be true and God tells us the same if we want and choose to do so. I feel in many ways I am just beginning to truly understand Significance myself.

Assumptions

In the writing of this book, I have based it upon a number of assumptions that serve as compelling reasons for putting my thoughts to pen; they are:

Today we live in a world where the family structure, makeup, and outcomes have become disastrous.

Our society and culture is a mess related to people's behavior and ability to interact with others.

Most have not learned how to live, interact effectively and be among other human beings.

There is so much struggle and recovery from bad stuff out there – a refocusing of our values is needed by many.

The technology/information age has driven us behind pieces of hardware instead of interacting with people. As a result, we have lost our confidence, desire, and interest in working and playing with others.

Everything has become about ME, the VICTIM, my EGO, my NEEDS, ISSUES, IDEAS, etc. This victim thinking is bad on so many levels. Forgiving SELF has even taken over as the predominant forgiveness dynamic.

My life overall, and specifically my last couple of decades working with organizations, teams, cultures, and PEOPLE reinforces to me that the principles of significance are not known or practiced by most.

People have a sin nature', whether you are a person of faith or not, this is real. It takes a constant focus to portray these principles well. Our instinct is to do the opposite in our minds and heart.

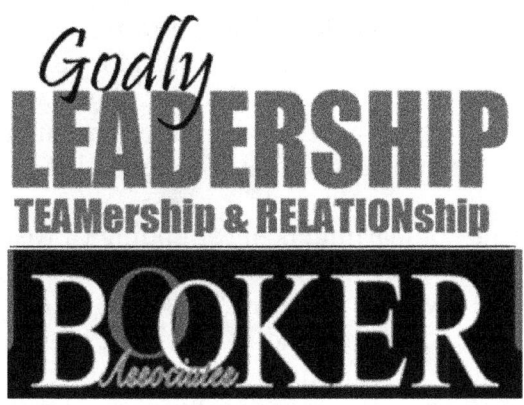

My love and passion for helping people grow are the true impetus behind writing this book. So many never learned the basics – for maybe most, no fault of their own. This book is about, starting now, getting back to the basics of what a good person is; how a good person should live. These principles are for you, those around you, and those you should be teaching.

> * This book is not intended to be a story, a textbook, a self-help motivational thing ...and is also not intended to be a preaching at you. It is not about me telling you what I am, but what I want to be!

This book is about significant pieces, random learnings and questions of practical life application to make us THINK. I love to *think* and I am sure you will find yourself deep in thought as you make your way through this! The information is meant to help you in your life, to challenge and motivate you to live in a more significant way, starting now.

As this endeavor evolved, I came to realize and will suggest to you here that this is good stuff for all of us; it is not only for you. The principles, values and walk described here would be a great mantra (or curriculum for learning) for any family, team, organization or sector of people.

Our journey of learning is never ending (if we choose to NEVER STOP LEARNING) - we are doing it together my friend! My wish is that this book will cause you to move and change, just by reading, thinking and personal reflection. I hope as well that we can actually find a way to help each other do it. After digesting, contact me, let's talk!

Doug Booker

Organization / Structure

After the sections on introduction, overview, and purposes, we get into the eight principles that demonstrate how we should live our life (how I believe we should...).

Within each section/principle I have included my general thoughts along with some advice, suggestions, and lessons learned.

Additionally, I have inserted quotes, scripture, and some leading questions. I wrap up each section with some dysfunctional aspects of the principle. These are intended to point out what one who doesn't practice the principle might look like, warnings, etc.

I leave you at the end of each principle with some Significant Questions. The questions and spaces provided throughout, will allow you to capture your thoughts. I believe you will be glad you did by the end, where you will be encouraged to create a personal assessment and develop an action plan for the rest of your life.

I have also included a few pages to explain my faith and beliefs regarding God, Jesus, and our Salvation.

<u>Defining – a beginning...</u>

What is Significance?

I think of Significance as being our Signature in this walk on earth, and beyond. How we live is our footprint that we leave by how we walk that walk. Some defining phrasing I have come across:

...the quality of having importance

...being regarded as having great meaning

...conveying quality; consequence

...the quality of being; with purpose

...the extent to which something matters

...making something matter

...impact, implication, adding up to, a sign of...

—This writing of this book is not so much about our purpose and
WHAT we are here for, but rather HOW we do whatever we are here for...! I would like you to consider that possibly the HOW *is* our Purpose.

> *So maybe you have already been leading a life of significance...*

Sometimes we come to life's crossroads and
we view what we think is the end,

But GOD has a much wider vision and
he knows that it is only a bend,

The road will go on and get smoother...and
after we have stopped for a rest,

The path that lies hidden beyond
us, is often the path that is best?

So rest and relax and get
stronger, let go and let GOD
share your load,

And have faith in a brighter tomorrow,
You have just come to a bend in the road.

-Helen Steiner Rice- I believe gets credit for this

...maybe not.

Maybe you are at a bend in your
Road to Significance.

Think about this. Any number of things could have preceded your reading this (divorce, a parent blowing you away with a comment, losing a job, losing it all in bankruptcy, failure on some level, dropping out of school, losing a loved one, betrayal, a dream gone wrong, or some other issue impacting your self-esteem).

Whatever it is, that does not define you —unless you allow it to do so. What you do from this point forward will be your signature, your significance! You ready to go round this bend in your road?

Getting Ready

Hopefully YOU are already doing some thinking; I know I am :). To get the most of this reading, I strongly encourage you to devote some concentrated time focusing on the key concepts of this book.

I recommend that if you have anything else going on around you (TV, Internet, music, etc.); either put this down and wait for another time or...

All quiet, distractions dealt with and focused now? Take a look below, I'll bet you have heard a few of these:

> **It's about the journey, not the destination...**
>
> **If you don't know where you are going, any path will get you there...**
>
> **It's not where you're from but where you're going**
>
> **If a man doesn't stand for something, he will fall for anything...**

So, what have you been doing, how are you doing it, and will you continue doing the same as you move forward in your life? Are you changing, growing, or improving in your walk?

<u>Somewhere I heard:</u>

...a rut is just a grave with the ends kicked out.

Where are you?

So how do we define greatness, (significance)?

He was a great man; and she was a great mother and wife.

She was an awesome boss and cared for her people.

He treated his wife like a queen.

He added to this world through his contributions to many worthy causes.

She taught school for 46 years.

A member of the church for 31 years – served people and a Deacon for 18 years.

His family truly loved him.

A Pillar of the community for several decades.

A Missionary to four countries spreading the gospel.

They were Foster parents for many years after raising three of their own children.

He raised five children on his own after losing his wife several years back.

She worked a regular job and served the Homeless Shelter three nights a week on top of that.

He worked tirelessly to help ex-convicts to find jobs; spent many weekends at the local jail counseling troubled folks.

Despite continual health issues, she did amazing things for the community and people.

??? She was always in a fight or argument with someone.

> Couldn't tell him anything, he knew it all!
>
> Never really got the hang of work, having a job, depending on himself
>
> She thought the world and everyone in it, owed her
>
> Always looked the other way when the offering plate slipped by
>
> She was a loner, liked to work all by herself; fact is no one could get along with her
>
> Selfish, materialistic, high ego – that was her life
>
> Died with tons of money, five people showed at the funeral
>
> Kept to Himself, never trusted anyone
>
> Would wear you out talking, but never cared much what *you* had to say
>
> Knew everything, always had an answer (everyone knew they didn't)
>
> Could never admit to being wrong, making a mistake, etc.

Surely SIGNIFICANCE is not behaving, acting, or walking in these ways?

MORE THAN A BUNCH OF ANTS:

In my times of pondering life, significance, and purpose - I sometimes picture all of us on this earth much like an ant colony. No really.

Stick with me here okay? Come on now, open up that learner (one of our principles here by the way) mind of yours and try to get this picture in your head. You are looking down on an ant colony from up above; got the picture? Can you visualize it?

All the ants are just scurrying around doing what they do. Do they have purpose other than their task of survival, eat, climb that wall, sneak in your house, building stuff, etc....? Note for you Ant Experts: If you know a whole bunch about ants, maybe you believe they do have purpose and significance. I am confessing right here, that I do not know much about ants. For our purpose here however it doesn't matter, the ant thing is just an analogy for creating this image and making a point! If you are an expert on ants, just let it go. If you have to discuss it, call someone. Go ahead do so right now. Close this book up, get it off your chest, and we'll see you back in a few minutes.

I will assume you are back and ready to visualize with me. So, you are looking down and seeing gillions of ants going everywhere. I think maybe that's how we appear from above. It is how I feel at times, like I am just scurrying aimlessly around doing LIFE; whatever that is for each of us. I remember being in this great spot high above the landscape in Ft. Collins, Colorado a while back. All I could see was (gillions?!?) of homes, buildings, cars, and people (ants☺).

There has to be more to what we are doing here than scurrying about... It may be good enough for ants, but not us. There must be more for me, and since you are still reading here, I will assume for you as well. We must have some important purpose we were put here for; at least I believe so.

If you are one who doesn't think about or aren't interested yet in the question of your significance and purpose - you probably don't need to read any further.

However, I am betting since you read even this far, you *are* ready and at least questioning stuff about your life.

That's where I want your head as you read this book – read, read it over again, find quiet moments, jot down some thoughts, question it, question yourself, discuss with others, take some action(s)...read on...etc.

I will assume that we are in agreement there must be some purpose in how we proceed on our journey of existence on this earth. So again, this book is about *how* we go about our lives day in and day out - whatever purpose or path you have chosen. There may be a faith component to this for you or not; either way, how we should be living is the point here. It is about how you live, function with others, and doing it all with significance. Maybe even magnificently!

> For when the One Great Scorer comes, to write against your name, He marks, not that you Won or Lost - But how you played the Game.

Grantland Rice (1880-1954), an American sports writer

I believe if you and I play *it* significantly, we will succeed in life; of course this depends how you view success. Maybe it is after all, how we play the game that truly matters?

What if we are here for a purpose other than a job, raising a family, a hobby or passion, going to work, driving here and there, fixing stuff, buying this, eating, solving problems, sleeping, ...scurrying, etc.?

Come now, you who say - Today or tomorrow we will go into such and such a town and spend a year there and trade and make a profit' - yet you do not know what tomorrow will bring... James 4:13

What is your life? Did you believe yourself to be in control of it? All we can maybe control is the application of these principles; how we walk our walk!

Maybe our purpose is about how we live our life – precisely just that and nothing more!

Just possibly, WHAT you do (job, hobby, passion) doesn't matter all that much in the larger scheme of things. This is not to discount the value and importance of being fruitful, working, and doing something productive in life. Being fruitful after all, is one of our principles, so yes; it does matter to have purpose in that sense.

SOME SELF-QUESTIONING:

It's time for a few questions. Do you have a pen/pencil ready? I have tried to leave space on our pages here if you are reading an actual book; otherwise for you e-readers, well you can figure it out.

In your opinion only, not considering what others think; capture some initial responses / thoughts to these questions. And, yes you have to!

What makes a good person?

What makes someone important?

What are the standards for fame and notoriety?

For what should we be remembered?

Is my treatment of others important; does it matter?

What matters, and what doesn't?

How do you know what to do to achieve significance?

As I look at others, how do I judge their significance?

In such a decaying world and society, to include the now dysfunctional family - how do you know what's right?

Aren't the Golden Rule & Ten Commandments enough?

What guides how you live, your standards?

What will get me to Heaven (if I am concerned about such things)?

What should our journey look like?

How does one know he/she is on the right Path?

What will you leave behind?

Maybe it makes sense that just as in our workplaces there is a job description; what should ours be as humans?

How will significance be measured when I come to the end of my road? What should I be practicing or doing to BE significant, or to achieve significance before my time is up?

What are the world's expectations? What are my own? ...and ultimately what are God's expectations for how we live our life?

We cannot change the cards we are dealt, just how we play the hand.
Randy Pausch

GENERAL THOUGHT:

Before I go on, let me again tell you, I am not here to dictate, decide for you, or otherwise preach at you. I am merely attempting to facilitate some thinking, learning, and questioning on a hugely important topic.

Periodically, as I thought, worked on, and wrote about the significance principles, there were moments when it seemed obvious and maybe even like common sense.

Very likely this will happen to you as well as you work through this reading. Trust the coach on this. Stick with it, we all need some focus on what's here! Everyone does not possess this stuff naturally, and neither do you in all likelihood. Yes, some you may have learned.

Consider this: If the principles do strike you as obvious and common sense - congratulations. You have, through experiences (teachers, parents, and other quality people in your life), learned how you are supposed to live your life. Since you are reading this, you must still be open to learning more though, huh? Maybe there are still lessons to learn or rethink ...

For the other 99% of the world, we never really clearly had these wisdoms of significance and purpose brought into focus. Much of this was just not learned; Likely, because we were never taught. The deterioration, breakdown, and dysfunction of family and our society are the result. Time to get back to basics...

Significance is not just about being nice; but clearly is a good beginning! Nice just doesn't assure these principles are happening.

The point is that these principles are learned (or not) by us in our lives. Many of us are missing much of this knowledge in the present day. The principles are behaviors, practices, and habits to be learned; they are *not* just common sense. These principles are not naturally how we are wired; without learning, constant focus, reinforcement, and practice. As a matter of fact, these behaviors pretty much go against human nature. Human nature is doing things in a *wrongful* way.

I believe this information can be life-changing. Life-changing for you and those around you; for this world and just possibly your eternal world. You may believe or not believe in eternal life, I understand that. For the record, I do believe in God, Salvation through Jesus, Judgment, eternity, etc. I want to be there with Him forever. That's just me☺.

>*Please know I am not here to convert you or try to win the -is there a God or not- argument with you.

I am sure that whatever side of God you are on, this book will be invaluable to you. The journey is about your significance and your life right here among the rest of us. This book is about our journey in this world of humans (or ants if you like).

MY OBJECTIVES: The book is...

Intended for those in my past, present, and future; so they may know what standard I am attempting to live.

Intended to share my knowledge, learning and beliefs with my own kids & of their families. To provide a starting point for assistance in raising & teaching my grandkids.

Intended for you and your children as well; those you now have and those still to come.

Intended also as an offer of knowledge for any & all young adults – the age when one is ready to move past life being about self only, accepting he/she does not know it all & ready to grow.

To be a re-focusing for anyone who has already been through seasons in life and is ready to really grab hold of being all they can be for their remaining time.

To share my beliefs in and about God & salvation; and what I believe His expectations are of us.

A Self-Help, Life Study, or Mentoring resource where growing self, others, and people in general is the goal.

For my Leadership Development work - for use in improving leaders, cultures, the management of organizations, and core values.

To provide new Believers (and mature ones as well) a plan for continued growth and good works.

To provoke improved thinking and behavior all of us.

To provide solutions related to the dysfunction and breakdown of our family and society – by improving the individual.

You judge for yourself.

At the end of this book, I will remind you and ask the question:

**<u>Do you see how adapting and adopting these principles in your life will lead to
Peace, Happiness and Significance?</u>**

PERSONAL INTENT:

Now, being somewhat around the beginning of my second half of life, I am compelled to get a better handle on significance. Not just for me, but for those (in my path) I may have the capability to influence.

For sure, I want to share pieces of the principles with loved ones. There are plenty of worldly resources and great books, to include God's Word / the bible and other faith works at our disposal to help us grow. My goal is to take what I have come to know and believe; extract and condense it all down to eight principles. I must tell you, I thought I could do this in 100 pages; didn't happen.

This set of principles is not perfect, just my best shot at the moment; my shot at starting here. You are going to add some great stuff to this list and make it even better. That's a good thing – I encourage you to further internalize and develop a learning tool to share with others.

STARTING HERE:

—It's never too late to be who you might have been.

George Eliot

Some GOOD NEWS to share as we begin. Issues in the past are in the past. This journey is about your significance from here on, your future. This very moment and every moment of your future is the focus. Regardless of how insignificant you may think of yourself or your life up to this point, this journey is all about SIGNIFICANCE Starting Now!

Maybe you see yourself as having been significant up to this point; that's great. How do you know? What was it based upon...? Regardless, we should **Never Stop Learning** (another of our principles by the way). Are you a learner?

Whether you are 19 or 99, the journey is about a significant finish! Maybe you feel there are some forgiveness issues (for example, one of our principles) that need to be sought out first. If so, go take those actions and then *move forward* my friend.

There may be any number of reasons why you have chosen to read this. I suspect as you progress through this reading, you will see (and feel) areas undoubtedly where you did (do) not do so well. I know I have experienced this as I wrote the book and must continue to work on those weaknesses and flaws.

*Move on from here! Past failures related to how we ought to have been as a human and one of God's children, are forgiven. I am saying so, and He says so as well, if we sincerely seek forgiveness.

More good news! The significance laid out here within these principles is about your Peace (which also happens to be our first principle).

Leading a life according to these principles will mean peace and happiness, this I totally believe. This does not mean there will not be struggles in life. There will be, I am sure of it. However it does mean that true peace and contentment will be the outcome of living a journey according to these principles. I am sure of this as well.

...Everything works out in the end; if it hasn't worked out, it's not the end.

Self-Worship vs...

If you are still in the season where life is all about YOU, just about YOU and YOU being first on YOUR list - then maybe put this away. No wait, if that is you, you need this☺, right now.

At some point we all *get* that life is more than just about *your* hair, how you will spend *your* weekend, finding excuses for all *your* woes, *your* latest drunk, sucking off of *others*, talking about *others*, *your* problems, opinions, *your* judgments, ...me, me, me - etc..... It is when we go from self-worship to other-focused or maybe even God-worship.

This may be hitting close to home. I am not trying to beat you up at all. Focus on Self as we will call it here, is a season of life *everyone* experiences. I will tell you that the quicker you can get through this me-season the better. Significance is likely not achievable as long as you are placing yourself first in this life. A focus on others or on something outside of *self* is instrumental in achieving significance.

It is a fact (in my opinion anyway) that there is more to this world and life than me ...you and your happiness. Can you deal with that? Trust me on this, real peace and happiness comes from a focus on others vs. self – more on this as we go along. Good news however, when you do focus elsewhere, you will find happiness.

It strikes me that this life is intended to be about who we are in ways that matter. I am reminded of the iceberg analogy – we see only 10% of the iceberg on the surface, while underneath is a very significant 90%. This 90% is where our real impact and significance is; not the external, visible, superficial you, but who you are down deep. That is the essence of this book.

For certain, there are people out there (and always likely will be) who have never moved past this season of Focus on Self. Maybe they will, maybe not. Maybe you can help them through that, maybe not?

How about just giving them this book and hoping (and praying for them)! That would be service (another one of our principles) to them by the way. Additionally, did you know (and this is another one of our principles) that we are to love those selfish ones and everyone else in this world?

At some point for all of us (I believe) – life begins to be about our questioning ourselves, how we are living, who we are, and life in general.

It is this wisdom I seek these days. You have likely heard something along these lines before; we all know down deep it to be true.

…When life is all said and done, it won't be about stuff accumulated; but about people, relationships and those we have helped, served, forgiven (or not). …about those we loved, and our workings in relationships. It won't be about possessions for certain; but possessions of the heart maybe. What you did in terms of people (others) will be what are remembered for it seems to me…

HEART & MIND

This book is about <u>our</u> mind and <u>our</u> heart. True significance can only occur and be achieved when we grasp hold in our minds and maybe more importantly within our heart. The journey is about who you are, not who you are pretending to be; it's not about playing a game so others will accept you.

It is not about putting actions or tasks in your daily planner or calendar, to ensure you get them done. A fulfilling life is about internalizing and becoming significant in your behaviors – your daily and lifetime walk.

It is about doing mastering the principles because YOU want to a significant person. With diligence, persistence, and commitment to improving self, soon you and I can BE-come these principles. We can BE-come significant - but it won't just happen naturally (which is why most of us have been through or are a mess right now).

In my 20 years of working with leaders in developing significant, sustainable, leadership practices - I speak to concepts and qualities such as caring, listening, involving, asking their opinion, teaching, giving feedback, etc.

Frequently comments arise such as, I just don't have time for this leadership stuff ...or words to that affect. As if some see leadership as an extra hour they have to add on to their day; extra actions they need to plug into their daily planner. An hour of significance maybe? ...that's messed up thinking! The leadership principles and practices are their job, and more importantly need to be who they are, what they are, and their leadership spirit walk.

In the same vein, to achieve significance, these eight principles need to become who we are and what we do – in your daily and lifetime spirit walk. If these behaviors are not who you are but just stuff you are doing insincerely, not from the heart - people will see through you in a minute.

...Let your purpose prioritize your life.

Luke 19:10 / Matthew 6:33

MAKING SIGNIFICANCE HAPPEN

How do we make these principles become _who we are'? For now, let me just say these principles are behaviors. If you have been *not* practicing the principles; the behaviors are *not* your habits (who you are). You have instead been practicing bad behaviors for as long as you have lived - these habits are not easily changed. Changing a behavior becomes an issue of accountability – you have to find ways of being held accountable. You cannot in all likelihood effectively change (BE-come these principles) on your own. If you were going to, you would have already huh?

Consider this: One does not, at an adult age of 30, 40 or 65 for example, say to him/herself _I am going to be a better listener' just because you read that somewhere. It doesn't work that way; and actually you already knew you were supposed to listen. You just weren't doing it, by choice.

By now these choices you have made in life (your behaviors and patterns) have become habits. It is who you are at this moment in time, what you have BE-come. You will need to involve others to hold you accountable to make these principles the new improved YOU.

If true change is to happen – we all will need to find partners, friends, mentors, spouses, church family, siblings, etc. to involve in changing yourself – maybe all of them! Give them permission to give it to you straight and to provide necessary feedback and critique. Oh yeah, you might also consider prayer. Ask HIM to help you with these and find out what HE says about this stuff. I will share some of that here, but much more is to be found in His Word (the bible).

* Now pay attention, this is critically important. If you aren't going to listen to these _accountability helpers', don't ask them. If you are going to instead just lash out at them and/or defend your flaws when noticed – don't even go there. It will be a complete waste of time if you aren't going to pay attention to the feedback. You, first of all, have to want to change and be open to

experiencing some difficult moments (growing pains) on the journey.

Ignoring, resisting, or defending your behaviors will also damage the relationship with the person you have asked.

This all reminds me of that ditty about there's one in every crowd. If you don't get that or there doesn't seem to be one in your crowd ...it might be YOU. Another twist on this – if everyone sees it the opposite of your way, there might be something there to pay attention to...

FAITH PERSPECTIVE

This research, study, and writing along with my personal relationship with Jesus have taught me that this journey is something bigger than just seemingly *doing the right thing*. Humans 'doing the right thing'- is not as easy as it sounds. Oh yeah, achieving significance is what God wants us to do as well. What I am going to share with you is what I believe to be biblically founded; and what I believe we are to BE; more in greater depth about My Faith is found on page 248.

For a second time, I am not trying to convert you.

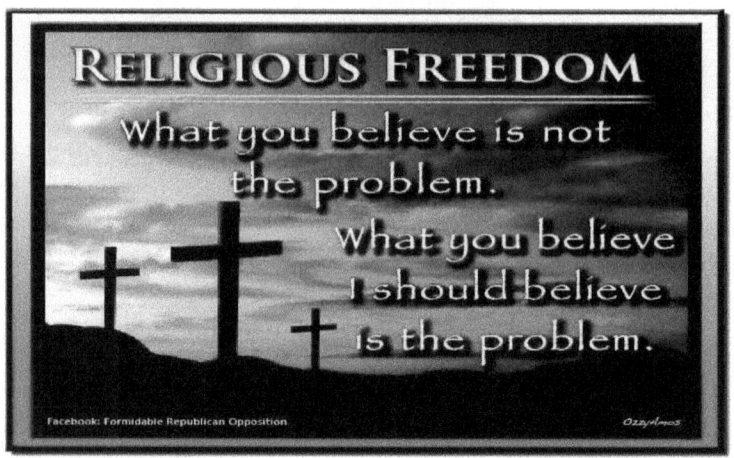

I just want you to know what drives me now; create some awareness and provide some foundation. Let me assure you that whether you are a person of faith or not – the principles will work for you. They apply in this world of people (with or without God in your beliefs).

Maybe you are just focusing on trying to improve and be the best person possible. If so, this is a good plan for you. The principles will lead you to significance; this I am positive. I am 100% sure that if someone were these eight principles, that person would be absolutely a significant person to me personally.

God is hugely behind everything I am saying here. Leave God out if you wish (I don't recommend it☺), but that is your choice. Maybe He will work on you as you read this; He does work on each of us in His own way...when you are ready.

*This book is not about denomination or religion. It is about - exploring and sharing what we should be practicing to become the most significant person possible. Again, not some perfect list - but at least a pretty decent path to follow for anyone. Take what is here, highlight pieces important to you, and toss in your own thoughts - and we might be real close.

Can I tell you also that attaining significance does not ensure a lifetime completely full of fun, happiness, good times, great health, wealth, and without struggles? The challenges will remain for each of us during our journey. Currently, no prescription exists for avoiding life's problems, issues, and challenging times. This book *is* about making the journey one of significance. Life will go on; the seasons will come and go. We will spend some time in the valleys, but there will be peaks as well. Realize, learn, and appreciate the journey by practicing and BE-coming these principles.

…Do not merely listen to the word, and so deceive yourselves. Do what it says. Anyone who listens to the word but does not do what it says is like someone who looks at his face in a mirror and, after looking at Himself …goes away and immediately forgets what he looks like. But whoever looks intently into the perfect law that gives freedom, and continues in it—not forgetting what they have heard, but doing it—they will be blessed in what they do. James 1: 22-25

Before totally leaving the faith aspect for those with interest, let me offer you some scripture as you seek wisdom. Maybe take some time right now to pray for your learning, acceptance, and patience.

Give me understanding…I will observe it with my whole heart, Ps 119:34

If any of you is deficient in Wisdom, let Him ask of the giving God who gives to everyone without reproaching or faultfinding, and it will be given Him. James 1:5

With the aged is Wisdom and with length of days comes understanding. Job 12:12

He who leans on, trusts in and is confident of his own mind and heart is a fool, but he who walks in skillful and Godly Wisdom shall be delivered. Proverbs 28:26

Weary not yourself to be rich; cease from your own human wisdom. Proverbs 23:4

Blessed is the man who finds wisdom, the man who gains understanding. Proverbs 3:13

Whoever obeys them (God's commands) and teaches others to do so will be called great in the kingdom of heaven. Mat 5:19

He who loves discipline loves knowledge; he who hates correction is stupid. Proverbs 12: 1

*Knowledge is information, facts, understanding, etc. Knowledge is good to have; however Wisdom is even better - that is the understanding of how to use the knowledge one has.

WISDOM

I am sure there was a season where I thought life was all about me; hopefully most of that is pretty much in the past. Another season most of us experience is when we believe that whoever is the smartest, or possesses the most knowledge wins.

Knowledge, data, and information are way over-rated (or at least trying to keep it all in one's head is...).

With the whole technology explosion, world-wide web, virtual world, etc. – knowledge of almost any kind is right at our fingertips. All that information these days is right there in our laptop, iPad, or even smart-phone. Anyone can go find knowledge, but knowing what to do with it once found, that's the challenge. That's wisdom. Einstein put it this way, (paraphrasing):

...knowledge is from the past, Imagination is the key,

I am adding... **Wisdom is the usage of that key along with that acquired knowledge...**

Significance and Wisdom are where I have interest these days. Here's hoping we all gain some wisdom in this focus on significance – that *would be* significant huh? Sorry, couldn't resist.

It only makes sense to me that our best model is not of other humans, great CEOs, great presidents, leadership gurus, etc.... Our model is the ultimately significant and perfect leader - Jesus.

We can all agree no one person will ever be 100% significant or perfect. Only Jesus can claim that. For sure am not and will never be. As hard as it may be to say - neither are you, nor will you ever be! I know this about you ☺ cuz I know stuff.

For the third time, I do not intend to preach at you from some almighty position like I know it all. That definitely is not the case.

Anyone who believes they are there - that they have learned it all, that they know it all – lacks wisdom and are not practicing one of our principles, LEARNING.

I hope, wish, and pray much awareness and learning may occur. I also hope we both will continue on with the lifelong pursuit of continued significant learning and growing toward our significance.

...People don't care how much you know until first they know how much you care (my favorite quote)

> Regarding this quote - I am also thinking here: God doesn't care how much you know either? Except maybe how well (much) you know Him!

BIG PICTURE / THE JOURNEY

Looking at life as Seasons is an interesting philosophical approach – to me anyway☺. Sitting here where I grew up and have returned (the Midwest) we know about seasons and change for sure. I wonder if there is any correlation with people from the Midwest being more adept to change. Hmm.... We know that hard times, storms, tough winters, or brutally hot summers are coming. We know also with certainty that when we are in those tough times, we are headed toward sunshine and blue skies –those beautiful Spring and Autumn seasons.

For certain it is in and through our seasons (or phases) of existence where we acquire wisdom; ...where we grow ...learn and change. It is through rough, tough, and painful seasons, which will be plentiful - where learning occurs if we care to dig deep enough to realize and accept it.

The following had to fit in here somewhere for me anyway - from Ecclesiastes (in that bible thing)................

A Time for Everything

There is a time for everything, and a season for every activity under the heavens:

A time to be born and a time to die,
   A time to plant and a time to uproot,

A time to kill and a time to heal,
   A time to tear down and a time to build,

A time to weep and a time to laugh,
   A time to mourn and a time to dance,

A time to scatter stones and a time to gather them,
A time to embrace and a time to refrain from embracing,

   A time to search and a time to give up,
A time to keep and a time to throw away,

A time to tear and a time to mend,
  A time to be silent and a time to speak,

A time to love and a time to hate,
   A time for war and a time for peace.

---

*Now, I urge you to go back above, and really read about each season to gain a bit of perspective on your past. Can you literally see where these changes happened? Can you pinpoint the learning that resulted? How did you change?

Peaks & Valleys

Most of us have also heard life addressed from the perspective of peaks and valleys. When we are in those deep, sometimes very dark valleys - we learn the most. Learning is about struggling – it isn't easy in life or in school even. Maybe when learning is happening, we should try to keep in perspective that we are climbing our way toward that next peak. In the same sense, likely when we are not struggling and all is smoothly going along - potentially little growth is occurring? Are you currently stagnant and not really learning or are you in the learning mode at this moment?

It is the unpredictable seasons (or valleys) that make life such a struggle at times. Significance is likely tied to our ability and capacity to realize that everything and every season is just a part of the journey; it will pass.

Are you able to focus on the journey, the process, and learning value; or do you get caught up in yourselves, focusing totally inwardly? Do you tend to fall into the woe-is-me, depressive, life-is-a-bummer mentality?

Wherever you are or whatever season you are in, it is heading toward a shift. It is just the way life happens - the way it all works! Predict what you can, and stay ready for change because it will come. Are you ready?

In the middle of adversity lies opportunity.
Albert Einstein

*If we can grasp this concept, there should be no real surprise when the shift(s) occur. Surely this way of thinking assists one in maintaining a presence of peace in his or her world. There's another of those principles, the first one we will be into in depth shortly.

Put another way - if it is good and you are on top, it is all currently smooth sailing - there is a valley likely headed your way. If you are in a valley, keep on moving forward because you are headed up again (believe it or not). Isn't that exciting, you are not only suffering, but you are learning if we are correct here☺.

Seasons do come and go – that's a no-brainer I realize. Failure, struggles, heartbreaks, etc. are a good thing ... IF we learn from them. It's kind of like the conflict dynamic I deal with in Leader Development. Conflict is a good thing – IF learning happens and we truly resolve it.

7 lovely logics:

1) Make peace with your past so it doesn't spoil your present.
2) What others think of you is none of your business.
3) Time heals almost everything, give the time, some time.
4) No one is the reason of your happiness except YOU yourself.
5) Don't compare your life with others, you have no idea what their journey is all about.
6) Stop thinking too much, its alright not to know all the answers.
7) Smile, you don't own all the problems in the world.

Our Principles

8 Principles of Significance. So we get into them finally - the eight principles.

As mentioned, I have provided you with some questions, scripture, quotes, identifiable connecting behaviors, and space for your thoughts.

As we delve in, I just want to re-emphasize the importance of the principles as a way to live. It's kind of interesting how we just sort of wing this stuff; assume and hope people know how to live right! Within our society, culture, a church or a family - what is the criterion for being a good person, a significant person? That's what we're doing here, trying to answer that question.

How do we measure a person? What's their worth, yours and mine?

At the end of the road, when you and I kick the bucket and go wherever you believe we will go, how will we be valued and measured? Now you will at least have a way or path, and what I believe is - The Way if you include God!

So here's my take and what we have determined to be eight criteria, factors, or principles for each of us to practice and master. Again, this is surely not a perfect list but is way than the vague, mushy perspective most plod along with in life. Your Significance Shift starts here.

PEACE

FORGIVENESS

SERVICE

LEARNER

TRANSPARENCY

THANKFULNESS

LOVE & RELATIONSHIP

FRUITFULNESS

It's not where you start, but where you finish…
(And I will add) **…and how & if you get there!**

> In my studies, I found this prayer, liked it and so decided to share it.
> Let this prayer of St. Francis guide your words and actions today.

Lord, make me an instrument of your peace.

Where there is hatred, let me sow love. Where there is injury, pardon. Where there is doubt, faith. Where there is despair, hope. Where there is darkness, light. Where there is sadness, joy.

O Divine Master, Grant that I may not so much seek to be consoled, as to console; To be understood, as to understand; to be loved, as to love.

For it is in giving that we receive.

It is in pardoning that we are pardoned, and it is in dying that we are born to Eternal Life.

Amen

PEACE

> **...I feel at peace when I have trust, respect, and no doubt about the genuineness of those around me. It is comfortable and leads to fruitfulness. Pride in one form or another seems to be the biggest challenge to our peace. It's not peaceful when I feel need to question their integrity; doubt his sincerity or her lack of transparency. Relationship and subsequently communication isn't good. That's stressful, worrisome, unproductive and exhausting.**

Readings I am working through at the moment have given me much to consider regarding this principle. For clarity – this is about the person; the peacefulness of a person, his/her peace in their life. This principle is not about peace of/in this world (although obviously there is plenty of connection that could be made).

A person of Peace is one who is at peace, comfortable in their own skin; focused on the present; good with Him/her(self) right now, at this moment, every moment.

This is the first principle for a reason. Although clearly to me, it is its own principle, it has much to do with how effective we are with the other seven! If we practice the other principles on a high level that might just equal a fair amount of peace? And vice versa – if one is a person of significant peace, he/she likely is practicing the other seven fairly well!

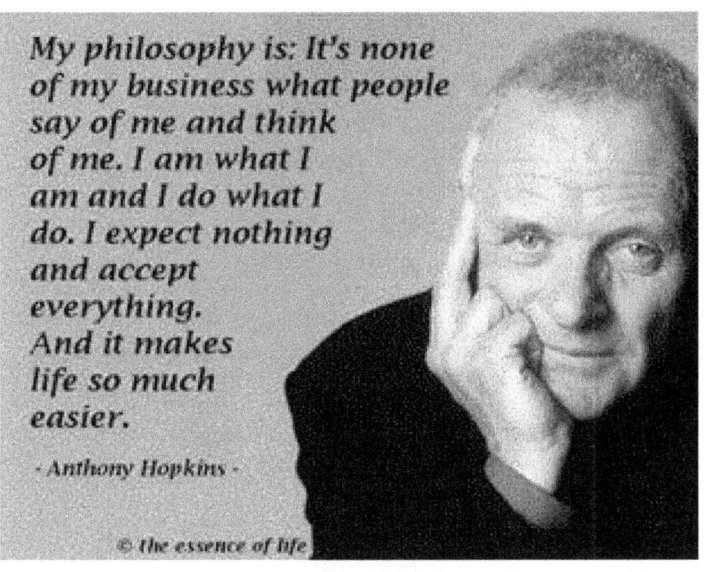

TRUST THE ANSWER:

Peace, in general, comes from trust. Trust that things are under control, you have done what you can, and now leave it with comfort and peace of mind. For those of us who know God, the person of peace will do what he can and put issues into His hands.

Peace, Peaceful, Peacefulness, and/or maybe Peacemaking / keeping – we find these undoubtedly in the individual who is truly doing life right. If one is leading and living a significant life, he/she has peace with self, with others, with God, etc.

When I think of such a person, I think of someone who doesn't get riled up at the least little thing that goes wrong. Peacefulness is flexible, open-minded, caring, and understanding of the importance of relationships.

A peaceful person is empathetic, accepting, and sees the bigger picture in everything. Understanding that everything is part of a process - the journey.

OUT OF CONTROL

I fear many and maybe most people in this crazy world of ours do not know the concept of peace. Let me take a shot at some clarification from my point of view and experiences.

We recognize the Peace factor in others as calm and accepting acts and behavior day in and day out. The peaceful person is under control in their daily journey. Maintaining that peace no matter what is going on around them. The peaceful person does not get overly excited, or get their day ruined at the littlest inconvenience or setback; making others around them more peaceful as well. Those who master peacefulness are also the Peace makers and Peace Keepers in our world. Helping in situations to keep things among people good. Unresolved conflict is not acceptable and is immediately dealt with, resolved.

You know the kind – quiet, mild, not a yeller or screamer; he or she exudes Peace. Even-tempered, calm and calming influence, speaks softly causing others to quiet themselves to listen. Obviously this is one who does not get caught up in arguing, fighting, etc.

*It doesn't mean the person won't fight for their idea, thought, value, or something important; but they will do so through a peaceful, tactful, and respectful exchange. They are rarely surprised by people and stuff in life!

You can't control your circumstances, but you can control your response.
Condoleezza Rice

THE PEACE OF GOD

Truly, I have discovered another level of peace in recent years, all because of God. A few years back, maybe much of life, I thought I knew peace; looking back I am not really sure I did. Going way back in my life - there was a stretch maybe between the ages of 12 to 17 (somewhere in there) when I know I felt peace. I was growing up in a Leave it to Beaver sort of existence – I think I knew peace. My parents were awesome; we had a good little life in a small town, after school/summer jobs, school, sports, girls, friends, and safe little small town environment. No real problems or issues - life was pretty darned good. I was a laid-back kid, maybe to a fault. However, as I look back, it was peace. I was peaceful, a peace-keeper, had great friendships and keeping things peaceful was a priority with me.

PEACE (or) HAPPY

I think I would have to say that was the most peaceful maybe I ever was until now. For clarity, let me say that this is not the same as happiness.

I do think **PEACE = HAPPINESS**, but not the reverse necessarily - hang with me here☺.

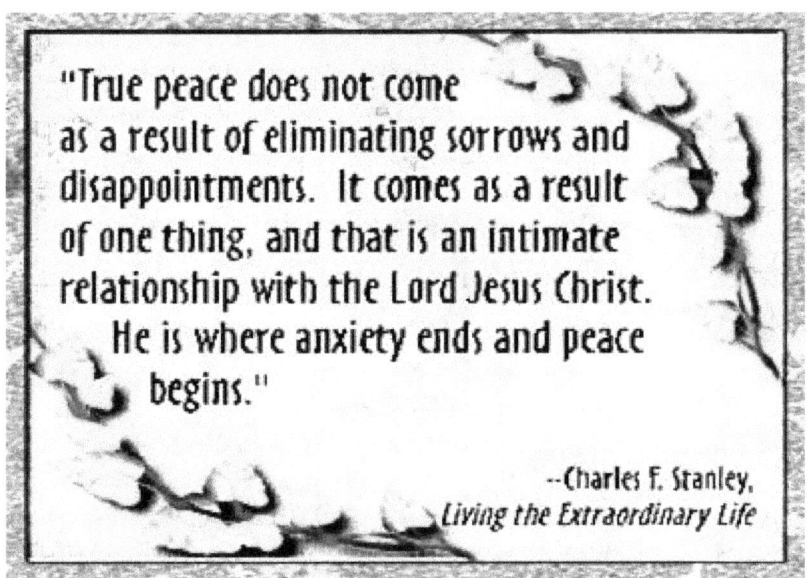

"True peace does not come as a result of eliminating sorrows and disappointments. It comes as a result of one thing, and that is an intimate relationship with the Lord Jesus Christ. He is where anxiety ends and peace begins."

--Charles F. Stanley, Living the Extraordinary Life

Here's what I think: My parents were providing that peace back then. I would even say that they were like my God to me; my parents were the ones providing, loving, forgiving, and teaching me. We did go to church pretty much every Sunday. However, as I think back, God was just an abstract concept I was aware of – but truly my parents were the ones I was really worshipping.

Move forward to the NOW. God is who I worship now; He is the one providing that peace for me now. Clearly it is a peace that comes from trusting in the only one we can totally count on in this life, Him!

Everything and everyone now takes a distant second place. Everything and everyone will be flawed, mess with my world, disappoint, be undependable, let me down, be imperfect just like me, etc.

Now, just as with all the principles, I am not nearly perfect with them, not even close in some cases. I am flawed like everyone else. I do not have total trust and I still do worry at times - this flaw is precisely why I don't have total Peace.

> As we grow up, we learn that the people that weren't supposed to ever let us down, probably will. You'll have your heart broken & you'll break others hearts. You'll blame a new love for things an old love did. You'll fight with your best friend, you'll cry because time is flying by, & eventually you'll lose someone you love. So take too many pictures, laugh too much, forgive freely, & love like you've never been hurt. Because every second you spend angry or upset, is a second of happiness you can never get back!

WORRY

My heart and mind tell me that if I did have complete trust in our Savior, I would not worry one little bit, ever! However, I am human, flawed, and imperfect, so I do worry, fret, and stew about stuff. Thus not 100% peaceful – however, I do have a bunch of peacefulness these days.

This is especially true as I write this book and focus on these principles. Consider what that means to us and the relevance of this discussion and focus on these significant principles!!!

With the level of peace I now have with Him, I am nearly 100% peaceful with brothers and sisters on this earth of ours. It just works this way for me; now people and stuff happening just do not surprise me or get me excited very often. I study and truly do love people; their flaws and imperfections are just accepted and understood. We are all knuckleheads on this level – you will mess things up with others and I may be one of those☺. I am also prepared that others are likely to frustrate me, let me down, or in some way screw with my world. When I expect it, I am prepared to deal with it – that's peace.

The bottom line, for me, is that I must place God as the number one relationship in my life.

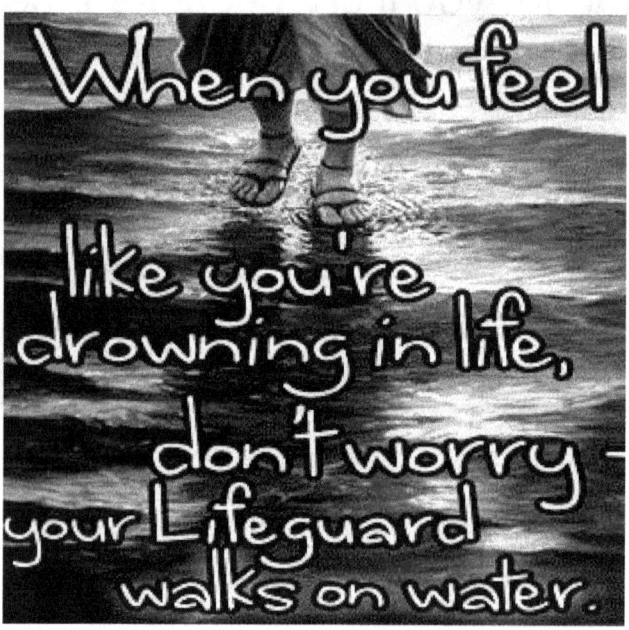

COMING HOME

You know that warm & fuzzy feeling we get after we have been away and return home? That peaceful, comfortable, cannot wait to be back; ready to de-stress and plop down in that comfy favorite chair, couch, or your own bed. You get it right?

On a recent trip, I had been praying for a lot of struggling in people's lives, and thinking how blessed I am. It struck me at that moment how that feeling of getting home resembles the feeling we get when we have God in our lives.

Amazing to think, but until I asked HIM into my life about a decade ago, I never knew that warm & fuzzy, peaceful, and loving feeling full time. It IS what happens when we ask Jesus into our lives. I know I thought I had that loving feeling, that I had it good, but nothing compares to where it is now. He sure gives me that feeling and knowledge of knowing He is always there. It is an instant thing, whenever I just think of HIM or say His name.

Even when we have our downs, struggles, and life problems, He is still there, providing that comfy, warm, & fuzzy chair, home-y feeling; like our Mommy or Daddy holding us. As the ultimate Father it is that same thing! But way better.

I am certain that no human can or will ever find 100% peacefulness without God in the picture. To try to achieve it without Him, with all of these flawed humans around us, we will always be let down, betrayed, negatively impacted, attacked........... Control what you can, don't worry, leave the rest to Him.

…Therefore I tell you, do not worry about your life, what you will eat or drink; or about your body, what you will wear… Who of you by worrying can add a single hour to his life? -O ye of little faith. Your Heavenly Father knows what you need. Seek first His kingdom & righteousness and all these things will be given to you. Therefore do not worry about tomorrow' Mat 6:25-34

WORRYING does not take away tomorrow's **TROUBLES,** it takes away today's **PEACE.**

NOT WORRYING is a tough concept for all of us, no matter who you are! Leaders have to (and must) deal with this personally as well as for those they lead!

In these challenging times with so much hopelessness, bad economy, people/friends losing jobs, organizations struggling, oil spilling, disasters here and there— who or what is next?

Will it be you, a loved one or some of those you lead? It is nearly a daily occurrence to hear someone close to us who has been impacted. I heard from a good friend and executive-level leader just this morning that is now out of a job. It's everywhere, and we're not supposed to worry?!? Indeed, this is one of the tougher biblical principles we are supposed to follow... YIKES, no that's DOUBLE YIKES.

DO NOT JUDGE

Spending time judging others will mess with your peace (fullness). It is useless, gains you nothing, stresses you out, and is just wrong.

…Judge not, that you be not judged. For with the judgment you pronounce you will be judged, and with the measure you use it will be measured to you. Why do you see the speck that is in your brother's eye, but do not notice the log that is in your own eye? Or how can you say to your brother, Let me take the speck out of your eye, 'when there is the log in your own eye? You hypocrite, first take the log out of your own eye, and then you will see clearly to take the speck out of your brother's eye.

Matthew 7:1-5

I personally came to put judgment into perspective last year or so when I connected it to the Golden Rule. As with so many other principles do unto others as you would have them do unto…'takes on a whole new meaning and importance when you replace others with God.

Do unto others as you would have God do unto…

If you judge people, you have no time to *love them.*
— Mother Teresa —

I don't think God exactly operates in this way, yet it is still how my heart and mind process this dynamic.

The point here for all of us is that we should just let people deal with themselves. Unless asked, their habits, behaviors, ways, and practices are none of your concern. Three exceptions I would suggest are:

> ...Leaders have an absolute responsibility to judge people (their performance as it pertains to their work).
>
> ...If you are asked for your opinion, viewpoint or judgment.
>
> ...Judging results, actions and outcomes of decisions from whence we learn.

...Don't speak evil against each other brothers and sisters. If you criticize and judge each other, then you are criticizing and judging God's law. Your job is to obey the law, not to judge whether it applies to you or others. God alone is the judge. ...so what right do you have to judge your neighbors? James 4:11

Where does judging begin or stop? We are about how someone fixes their hair, bias, discrimination, how people eat their food, brush their teeth, drives, walks, looks, thinks, reasons, acts, etc. It is controlling and is so not your business or your job! How often have we heard (or muttered these words ourselves): It's none of my business, but... We just need to shut up huh!?!

How you would do (I) 'vs... Them? Whether we are speaking of another person's attributes, habits, or sins; our judgment about them drives us crazy and out of peace! We are all so different because God made us that way – not your way. Are you in a position to criticize God's work? I heard a while back about how we all tend to sort of rate sin; we overlook our own but view other's sins as the bad stuff. These dynamics cause churches and Christians to be viewed as hypocritical. Not being hypocritical in this regard are you?

Counting other people's sins does not make you a saint

A critical spirit is like poison ivy, it only takes a small contact to spread its poison.
    God's Little Devotional Book (...and one of the seven things God hates – Gossip)

Gossiping, spreading rumors, etc. is something in my leadership work I deal with well. I tend to refer to gossip as COMMUNICATING MESSAGES TO THE WRONG PERSON!

We've all seen it...done it...and had it done to us as well! If you gossip now, stop. Groups, teams, and cultures can be destroyed by it. This destruction goes on all the time, stopping it will result in increased teamwork, trust, less conflict, more productivity, and improved relationships all the way around.

Stuff to understand about gossip; here's a situation: You have a problem with someone (what they said, what you thought they said, their opinion, something they did that impacted your world, something you judged them on, etc....get the picture?

What do we typically do when this occurs? We go share it with someone else—a peer, a boss, everyone except the person who really needs to hear it! Teammates / employees within the same office frequently will even take it straight to the leader. Think of the impact and fallout of doing things this way:

> First of all the person you are taking it to can do nothing but listen to your bellyaching....what are you expecting them to do with it?
>
> If they go do something with it, then they have broken your trust!?!
>
> If you allow them (or push them to do it for you) all you are going to do is lose respect and your relationship with *that* individual.
>
> What do they now know about you and how you will deal with things when issues come up between the two of you?

> **Be careful who you trust. If someone will discuss OTHERS with you, they will certainly discuss YOU with others.**

We all have our gripes with each other for good reason, but why don't we agree to start doing things in the right way in the right spirit, in a transparent way...?

Take it to the person in question. After all, if you tell me what your issue is or what you don't like that I did, say, or whatever - haven't you actually done something positive regarding the improvement of our relationship?

The gossiper tends to take confrontation and disagreement as world-shattering stuff instead of the good that is to be gained. However if we can manage to handle confrontation in a respectful, tactful, and non-blaming way, things have changed, improved, become better.

Gossiping and gossipers are Peace-destroyers. Tearing down relationships, impacting communication, morale, killing trust, and making life miserable for all around the issue. Not to mention all the wasted time that occurs ...because we took it through a cycle and circle of the wrong people.

Blessed are the peacemakers; for they shall be called the children of God. Mathew 5:9

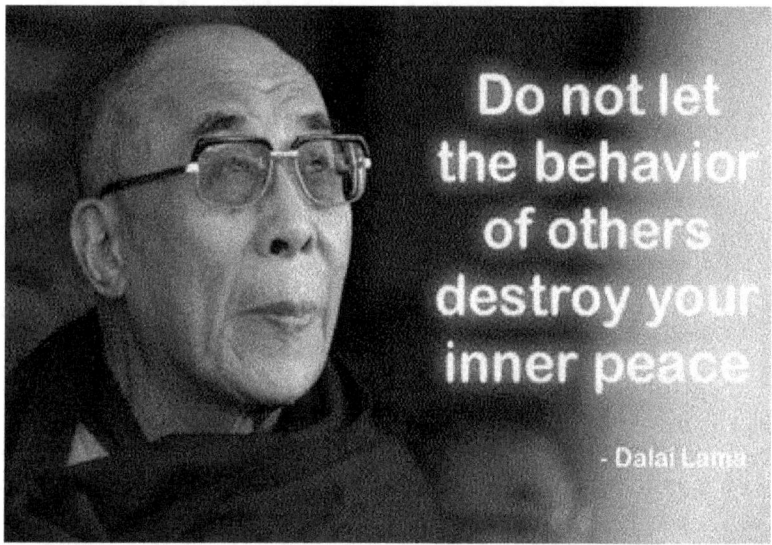

> ***Note:*** At the end of each principle section, I will leave you with some thoughts and words regarding what a person, who doesn't practice the principle, might look like.

DYSFUNCTIONAL **<u>Peaceful</u>** DYNAMICS

A person lacking peace is one *reacting* to everything; likely unexpectedly and negatively since he/she is not in control of their life. Chaos, troubles, and issues surround them and are linked to a constant dialogue about all the stuff happening to them. Problems go on and on as they are never really resolved, but excuses and blame are spewed as if nothing is their fault. Blame is the reasoning for everything. These people are superficial, non-learners, and all knowing. The lack of peacefulness is also clearly portrayed as worry – full of bad luck coming their way, impending doom, and fretting about what's to come. This person is for sure the kind that would stir people up negatively; sharing about others and judging their actions and behaviors; Oblivious to their own faults and failures. Everything would be about them; no care or concern for others issues, needs, or wants. Anger and frustration likely would be their mantra. Bad relations, few friends, and those who are around them are just as bad or someone who takes pity, listens, and likely even enables their behavior.

Other words that come to mind of a person lacking peace in life: conflicted, prideful, jealous, yeller, screamer, anxious, grudge-bearer, high drama, one who covets....

We have all known or do know people who exist in turmoil. I have known a few who just seemed to thrive on creating chaos, enjoyed the craziness caused by a lack of planning maybe... I am sure it was the attention it brought to themselves that they liked.

Anyone or anything come to mind at this moment:

SIGNIFICANT QUESTIONS ON PEACE:

1. Are you miserable? What's it about and how do you fix it?

2. When things get crazy, what do you do to get re-grounded (at peace again)?

3. Where do you find peace in your world?

4. What would peace feel like if you could achieve?

5. What are the obstacles / barriers in your life keeping you un-peaceful?

6. All dressed up ready to go, on the way, you get rear-ended and it's 97 degrees outdoors; what happens to you?

7. What could you do about these obstacles (causes of un-peacefulness)?

8. When did you feel peace in your life (if ever); what did it feel like?

9. How do you cause peace in other's lives?

10. Do you or others around you stir up worlds by gossiping and spreading negative information?

11. When was the last time you were really angry; does it happen much?

12. When things get truly crazy, who do you call? (If you don't have such a person in your life, go develop a couple. One will never be enough for everything)

13. How will you bring more peace into your daily life, beginning now? Who could help you?

14. Do you find yourself worrying and stressing over stuff?

15. Moving forward, how will you measure and achieve significantly more Peace in your world(s)?

FORGIVING

> ...Forgive those who insult you, attack you, belittle, talk about you or take you for granted.
> Forgive him. Even if they do not care, she is not sorry or he didn't ask for your forgiveness. Forgive her. Not doing so damages ourselves in so many ways.

A New (Golden Rule) Perspective

As I mentioned within the previous principle's discussion, I realized not too long ago some clarity about the Golden Rule that just never dawned on me before. What I realized was the rule applies first of all to you and the relationship between you and God!

Do unto others as you would have GOD do unto YOU. Think about this: If I want God to forgive me, I must first be willing to forgive others. If I want to be forgiven, I must be a forgiver. If I am not going to forgive Joe, Sally, etc., then guess who isn't going to forgive me?

Forgiveness is something most everyone struggles with, of this I am sure. Know that this dynamic is hugely a matter of the heart, not just the mind.

This isn't just the mind telling us that we should forgive, so we more or less try to cut Him or her some slack. This is about truly letting go of the hurt and pain caused and really forgiving someone for their actions.

Maybe even about hoping, praying, and wishing good things for that person?

And oh yeah, meaning it!

Forgiveness - the Benefits

Forgiveness is a positive in so many ways. Forgiving is a liberating, life-returning event.

> Forgiveness is a promise not a feeling. When you forgive other people, you are making a promise not to use their past sin against them.
>
> *Jay Adams*

Forgiveness is tied to such things as peace, happiness, contentment, love, as well as stress reduction for sure! When we are caught up in hurt feelings and focusing on something someone did that we cannot forget - we are in a bad, dark place. Not forgiving or carrying a grudge (or however you want to phrase it) is all consuming and self-destructive, stressing the mind and body, wearing us down. Not forgiving makes us dull and unfruitful playing out in conversations and interactions with others; dominating our mind without consciousness.

Besides the emotional toll of stress, no one wants to be around you when you are bearing a grudge, criticizing others and what I call dogging people. Likely, anyone that enjoys being around someone who is consumed anger and hate, is someone who is living with the same stuff. Forgive, and help those hanging around you do the same.

It clearly seems okay and maybe even logical to feel negatively when someone does something to us. They deserve our anger, don't they? Well here again, if we want to be forgiven, we must first be forgiving. Have you always deserved forgiveness from others, from Him?

The Peace we Gain

Forgiveness is not just for human, worldly peace of mind; but also what God tells us to do. You want to be good with HIM don't you? Well, if the answer is ‚yes', you better get right with the perpetrator (that person that did that bad thing to you). As a follow up and to be accountable to make forgiveness stick, try telling others good stuff about the perpetrator. You will confound all those who you have been sharing your negativity with; they will take notice of your change of heart. Now you can teach them about *this* journey you are on.

I can tell you that I am for FORGIVENESS

I have so much I need forgiveness for; I cannot afford to not be a forgiving soul. If I don't forgive, I am so going to pay. This I believe.

My two kids, now adults with families of their own, have so much they could hold against me because of what I put them through during their childhood. I was a crummy father to them during a season (or two) of their lives. I am sure there was a period where my kids held things against me. I believe my kids have let their anger go. I do not think I deserve to be forgiven, but they have and I am so very thankful. I am sure (positive) they will never forget, as I know I won't.

Totally forgetting is impossible I think, we are human and unless dementia or Alzheimer's sets in, those feelings are there for the long haul. If we forgot, then we couldn't learn from mistakes, bad experiences, etc. The forgiveness thing is about the heart.

Forgiving Self?

I believe I mentioned self-forgiveness earlier, but will expound just a little here. In res3earching the concept of forgiveness, I kept coming up with this forgive self-first. On some level, I am sure this is an important dynamic, therapeutic method and need. At the same time I just wonder if the concept isn't more of this ME generation we are in, where everything is about ME.

I know there are some who will take issue with my theory, as I am sure self-forgiveness is a popular counseling concept. I sort of think that concept as a load of #@!!... Forgiving myself?!! I could be wrong here, and if so, If I have offended or bothered you in some way with my interpretation FORGIVE me will you?

We will delve into some of these issues and concepts deeper in the ‗Service' principle; I won't go into much more here; only to say life is good when we focus outside of ourselves and onto others. The first *other* is God for me, but that's your call who you place first!

The best way to go from bitter to better - is to get rid of the (I, me…)

If you want it …give it

Forgive others, seek their forgiveness for your mistakes and sins against them, and leave the self-thing to God. God will forgive you, just ask – and then get back to a significant principled life focused on others and move forward. You don't get to forgive yourself, only others that need your forgiveness. Do that now if you have not previously. Then let others forgive you as necessary (if they choose) and the rest is up to God …if you seek that!
I heard an interesting little pointed-story a while back about _forgiving and forgetting'. Consider the difference especially in those situations where you are hard pressed to say you have forgotten. Maybe you have essentially gotten past the anger, you have forgiven, but have you forgotten? Likely, it is part of just being human that we don't forget. Maybe that's actually a good thing since the inability to forget probably ties into our _learning logic'. Anyway back to the ditty…

There was a little catholic girl who had been to a non-denominational church camp and had come back fired up about the Lord. She was talking excitedly to her priest one day and was sharing about how she communicates to Jesus all the time now. She told him of how when she does something wrong, she gets forgiveness directly from God if I just ask and seek it in my heart through Him. The priest was a bit surprised with this as the Catholic religion practices people confessing (passing info) through the priest.

Pursuing this a bit, he asked her if she had done something wrong, would she come to him to confess and she explained there is no need since we can all now talk directly to God.

The priest getting a bit irritated and upset decided to challenge her and her ability to communicate to God directly. He told her that during his seminary days in college he had done something wrong and next time she talked to Him, if she would see if He would tell her about it. She said sure.

In their next encounter after listening to her talk about her relationship and communication with God still going so well, he asked her about his question.

So did you ask Him about my wrong during my college days?

She responded, Yes I did. After asking what it was, she explained back, He said he had forgotten!

…Do not seek revenge or bear a grudge against one of your people, but love your neighbor as yourself. I am the Lord. Leviticus 19:18

DYSFUNCTIONAL **FORGIVING** DYNAMICS!

I think of the non-forgiving person as judgmental, self-righteous, and egotistical; wow that was strong huh? We have all been unforgiving at moments in our life haven't we; did that make us all these above, yikes!

Maybe it did on some level. An unforgiving person is also likely to be an opinionated, insecure, non-learner. The un-forgiver would likely be someone who has to be right, and is always to be blamed. I would also comment, as, I look at each of the principles, I notice how closely interlocked and connected each are. Being bad with one or two principles starts to look like the same kind of person – miserable, judgmental, bearing grudges, etc. It only makes sense actually that if someone is un-PEACEFUL, he/she is also likely un-FORGIVING and/or vice versa; Someone who always worries about the wrongness of others vs. their own issues, flaws, and imperfections. I would also guess many who might fall into this category, might be totally shocked at someone not willing to forgive them!

Other words that come to mind for the un-FORGIVING: bitterness, unmerciful, not sympathetic, not tolerant, not lenient or willing to cut anyone some slack for making mistakes...

> **Anyone or anything come to mind at this moment:**

SIGNIFICANT QUESTIONS ON FORGIVING:

1. Is there anyone in your life who seeks your forgiveness?

2. Whoever it is (was), when are you going to forgive them?

3. Would your forgiveness of someone help you?

4. What does holding a grudge or not forgiving someone do to you?

5. When others see you not forgiving someone, what's the message to them about you?

6. Did someone who you respected, a believer maybe, ever do anything to you that you haven't forgiven them for?

7. How would giving or receiving forgiveness change your life?

8. Why don't you call him or her right now and deal with it?

9. Is there something you did long ago, that you still feel guilty about, but have never shared with anyone?

10. For that person(s) in your life who did something to you, can you still love them?

11. What happens to you when you are consumed about someone else and their behaviors, actions, mistakes, etc.?

12. Do you buy into the concept of unconditional love ....or is your love conditionally doled out?

Is there someone in your network or circle you have wronged?

13. Is there a difference between forgiving someone in your mind/ heart and doing so in person?

14. Can you think of people who hold a grudge and never can forgive others – what do you think of them?

It may not always be the easiest thing to do, but it is always the right thing.....

SERVICE

For I was a hungered, and ye gave me meat: I was thirsty, and ye gave me drink: I was a stranger, and ye took me in:
Naked and ye clothed me: I was sick, and ye visited me: I was in prison, and ye came unto me.
Then shall the righteous answer Him, saying,
Lord, when saw we thee a hungered, and fed thee? Or thirsty, and gave thee drink? When saw we thee a stranger, and took thee in? Or naked, and clothed thee?
Or when saw we thee sick, or in prison, and came unto thee?
And the King shall answer and say unto them,
Verily I say unto you, Inasmuch as ye have done it unto one of the least of these my brethren, ye have done it unto me.

Mat 25:35

I believe this principle is about having a heart and focusing on <u>others over self – bottom line!</u>

My worst time(s) in life, in every sense, was when I was focused on myself, my problems, issues, and woes. When we place others over ourselves, to include their problems and issues – we will find peace and happiness. I'm telling you it works. Realizing this came way late in life, and I have also come to know it to be a God-thing (like everything is). We are doing Godly work when we are serving.

* Do I truly care about others problems, baggage, etc.? Caring about others is really what this whole SERVICE-thing is all about, to me anyway.

As I perused pictures depicting the topic of service, giving, etc. – it was funny how so many used dogs as the focal point.

As I pondered, it struck me that dogs are that way, unwavering loyal; always there for you no matter how you treat them; at your feet where Jesus showed us much about service in washing disciples feet... It is having a heart of service, a heart focused on others.

I am telling you, just like the first two principles, I come back to that Golden Rule dynamic. Do unto others as you would have done to you – by others and/or by God. Take care of His people and He will take care of you. I so believe that to be true. Again (like all the principles) this is heart-stuff.

You know people that are service-oriented - they focus on others above and beyond themselves. On a practical level, that is what service means to me, a concern for others as a top priority in our life. A person of service is one who gives, helps, reaches out, and asks others their opinion first. The service oriented person will sacrifice for others, not concerned of whether or not someone deserves the forgiveness. He/she loves people and wants to be there for them. This is not about being ‗Mother Teresa', but having this kind of heart, and mindset.

Without making this a downer comment in the midst of this, I must remind you there is a dysfunctional aspect to this principle in extreme cases.

The servant heart can be used (abused) by others. The servant heart can be enabling to others. As mentioned again, I am not saying this from the standpoint of whether or not someone deserves your giving. I am just sticking this thought in here to create awareness that giving can become twisted; and become enabling and destructive to that other person. I wrote some on this further on page 219 in our principle of Love & Relationship.

…not looking to your own interests but each of you to the interests of the others. Philippians 2:4

From a purely human-to-human point of view, a service-principled individual: opens the door for others; let the person exit the elevator before trying to get on; let others speak first demonstrating your *wanting* to know what they think or believe. Service-oriented people have a YOU FIRST mentality. It is knowing that serving someone requires manners, respect, and possessing good will toward other people.

This person would stop to help someone in need; he/she would likely pull over at one of those road intersections where someone is holding a sign asking for help. He/she is there to bless others.

✷✷✷✷✷

Did you ever stop and hand money to someone on the street begging for money? Should you? If not, did you not because you were judging them? Maybe they are not going to buy liquor with that money? Maybe the situation really is about YOUR service and giving heart and THEIR thankful and appreciative heart.

Maybe this act is just a God-thing placed in your significance path? Maybe it is not about us guessing how they may (mis)use your offering, but it is about your offering!

A significant person is one of God's people helping God's people. The servant individual knows that when he gives and serves others, God is looking down thanking the individual for helping one of His.

When life is at its very best, I am focused outside of ME... onto others!

If you are focused on others by giving, serving, etc. – you are taking care of you as well. You gotta' like that concept huh? You are receiving after all!

When I place others above myself in importance, this is BE-ing humble. Humbleness is not self-serving. Humbleness is clearly aligned to the principle of service (helping, giving, etc.). It's the same - just different (always liked that phrase, so true but funny).

I think at first glance, humbleness seems to be a weak behavioral thing. I think maybe most consider it as weak, meek, mild-mannered, never talking, low self-esteem, etc. I am not sure where that thinking comes from, but the spirit of being humble is not that at all. The significant person realizes humbleness is not just strength, but a position of strength. Some would say a Servant Leader quality trait is *Humbleness*.

Humbleness is perhaps the opposite of ego (egotism). When we think of being egotistical, we think of self-serving. We think of everything being all about me, we think of us first and foremost in this life. Maybe we have that one wrong also. Maybe high ego means confident, strong, secure, etc. Just trying to get you thinking outside of your box a bit here.

******

Some concepts and thinking that will hopefully make you go hmm...?!?

>My self-worth seems best (seems weird) when I focus on other's troubles.
>
>The company or customer service representative (there to focus on others) sharing his/her troubles vs. taking care of the customer?
>
>Service is the essence of Servant Leadership right? How do you and/or your boss view this? Is a leader to serve or be served?
>
>How easy it is to focus on others when we are in the judging mode? Indirectly, judging others is actually a focus on self. It is easier judging others than ourselves huh?
>
>I heard a parenting radio show about the latest thinking on kids; about constant praising and intent on building self-esteem actually becoming very damaging. This technique actually teaches the child that everything is about (them) YOU!
>
>The service principle reminds me of my days as a military commander. The expectation was when we were eating a meal - the soldiers ate first. Leaders went last.
>
>Leaders helping (and doing their job) facilitating the resolution of a conflict between two people; he/she has done a great thing serving them and the team.

Our society, workforce, work ethic, and just generally people working together is challenged these days because of a real focus on self. It is an all-about-me generation??!

When the elevator opens, do we rush in or wait for others to come out? When we are in a discussion, conflict, or argument - do we listen first?

Before you, the leader (or any leader), makes a decision, do you see what *they* (the team) think first?

When we (employees) are focused on the team's troubles, we are much more satisfied, motivated, and have a sense of belonging.

This all touches on that **THROWING STARFISH** story (you've heard this huh?

> *...about the person wandering the beach, picking up starfish and throwing them back in the sea before they die on dry land. Someone challenges how this can't possibly make a difference with all the many starfish on the beach. The person responds with, tossing another out into the waves... saying, it will indeed make a difference to this one.*

<u>*I guess this would clearly be a significant person huh?</u>

STORY...   Before finishing here, let me share a lesson I have learned regarding the value of focusing on others. This is a leadership lesson I gained from a personal experience during my days in the military. I'll make this quick – so, there I was, as a fairly new officer in the Army Infantry... I had done something good. It was one of those few occasions when I did something special, actually something exceptionally well (to be honest I have no clue what I did). Let's just pretend it was amazing... Anyway, I can still about 30 years later, remember walking down a sidewalk with my Commander, and approaching was his boss and our Battalion Commander. What happened at this time made such an impact on me about valuing others, praising others, real leadership, and service even. In speaking of something that the unit had done well, my commander threw all the credit on me for making it happen. He could have taken, but he gave me the credit instead.

Now surely I did it, but how many leaders would do that? He didn't have to; yes he should have, but he didn't have to... This act made such an impact on me – not what

I had done, but what he had done. He had just done something very significant.

I will let you digest that here. Now go ahead, first of all, as we all tend to do – process it as the victim at times where this wasn't done to/for you. More importantly, how do you do in those roles where you represent my commander's servant heart, that day?

In your life, do you throw the glory upon others? More importantly do you throw it upon God? I believe all this is about service - serving, a servant heart, and the focus on others first, etc.

How's your heart and mind about all this?

…God won't give us more before we are faithful with the little things. Luke 8:16

…For everyone to whom much is given, of Him much is required. Luke 12:48

DYSFUNCTIONAL **SERVICE** DYNAMICS!

Service is at the very core of significance to me – is our focus on ourselves or on others?

The person, who is not significant in service, is someone who remains in the -what about me- world, their world. Life is about themselves first and everyone else a distant second.

We will see this attitude in actions, behaviors, and conversation. They will want to insert their opinion and thought first of all, and maybe (not likely) but maybe then be interested in yours...

If you are sharing a candy bar, they will have never grown out of that –gimme, gimme- stage and will grab quickly the bigger half.

Likely, this is someone raised in this manner, where all the focus and limelight was thrown on them. They were enabled, they were constantly told how great they were, and they bought it, in spades! Thank you is never in their dialogue although, they will take and seek to be given to, as we have stated here.

Words that resemble the person lacking SERVICE:

Selfish	Not thankful
Egotistical	Arrogant
Self-centered	Tight
Judgmental	Materialistic
Self-worth inflated	No time for others
Acknowledging others (not)	Isolated
Stingy	Thief

Anyone or anything come to mind at this moment:

SIGNIFICANT QUESTIONS ON SERVICE:

1. Is giving an easy thing for you; is it conditional?

2. Is service or serving placing yourself below others ...or how do you see it?

3. Who or what was the last individual (entity, cause, organization, etc.) you helped?

4. Does intent matter in regard to serving, helping or giving to others?

5. When you see someone on the side of the road (someone asking for money at an intersection or a hitch-hiker) – what are your thoughts?

6. Is helping or giving to someone like helping God (in your mind)?

7. Has anyone helped you get to where you are today (did you thank them ....yet)?

8. Is there anything that you do that helps your community or mankind in general?

9. Have you ever participated in a community effort of helping and giving?

10. Is anything to be gained by serving others?

11. Would you rather receive or give?

12. At the end of a long day following dinner, you and your significant other are sitting relaxing. The idea of ice cream hits you both – are you going to get up and go get it or allow Him/her to?

13. Is there someone(s) you admire that gives and helps others freely?

14. Do you know others who give too much and are taken advantage of maybe?

15. Is there someone(s) you have helped along their journey?

DO IT NOW.

**SOMETIMES
'LATER'
BECOMES
'NEVER'**

*So what do your responses (above) suggest about your significance regarding the Principle of Learning?

Are you a Learner? I have been in / around learning for most of the last 25 years. These experiences have been in roles of teacher, consultant, coach, and university faculty member. I can tell you learning is a huge issue (problem) with many, and maybe most in our society. I have plenty of thought regarding the cause, but you are just going to have to run me down later to go into all that. For now, let's focus on YOU and your significance as a LEARNER.

Instead of being there to learn something we don't know about, most are there sitting in the student's role (or in a workplace meeting) trying to prove how much they do know. You have to let this soak in and really ponder this thought for a moment to get the point – and benefit to you if you can grasp it.

STORY... Before going on, let me share with you a story of learning and well let's call her, Susie. This might just be called the story that led to the fallacy many try to spout about no question is stupid. Yes, there is absolutely a stupid question, and we all have asked at least a few of them – leading to at least part of the problem with learning today.

This principle is about how we do this learning-thing so wrong in so many ways from Day ONE in our early seasons of life. (By the way, if Susie is your name, change the Susie in the story to some other name).

Go back or at least try, to day one of your kindergarten class. Picture the setting– boys in new jeans, girls in new dresses, wired and excited about all the stuff they have been told about. They have been pumped up about learning new things, meeting new friends, doing fun things, etc. Got it? They are all ready, all 20 little knuckleheads (just a term of affection for all of us on this earth☺). All getting ready to experience their first real taste of TEAMS and LEARNING

<u>Here it begins; the teacher asks the first question.</u> Remember this is the first question in the first hour of your very initial experiences with LEARNING and TEAMS.

And here is where it all begins to unravel – the value (and fun?!?!) of SCHOOL, GROUPTHINK, LEARNING, TEAMWORK, etc. Here is where your significance as a Learner began to take shape.

Back to that first question; teacher now unknowingly begins to start messing them up in their learning quest. The kids are wired and excited as they all think they know the answer.

[So a question for you, the reader: how many raise their hands? Think about it, not as you are now, but as you were way back then, before you learned what you now know.]

You are absolutely correct, likely ALL of them raise their hands because they do not know what you and I know. This is not going to be FUN for the person who gets chosen and has the wrong (stupid) answer huh?

Teacher calls on Susie. Susie proudly throws out her best response, what she believes to be THE answer, only to find out, this is something she doesn't understand, didn't learn yet, picked up somewhere erroneously, whatever... Regardless, she is WRONG.

With this wrong answer, what do we all know occurred in response (from the team mind you)?

She was laughed at, as natural reaction by many, and probably by a few because they are just mean (already).

Teacher, (like most in leader roles, with little to no real understanding of leading, facilitating, or the impact of such a thing on Susie's future life) just allows the reaction. Susie is demoralized while teacher encourages the kids to get quiet, back under control, and teacher moves on...

Now, what do we know about Q#2? Right you are again, Susie ain't playin... no more and neither is anyone sharp enough to figure out already that getting laughed at if you are wrong isn't fun. Not knowing the right answer has now become a threat, an opportunity to look foolish, to be laughed at, and heaven forbid, to be wrong. There is a stupid question (or answer) and I just gave it, thinks Susie and others.

I would normally go forward through the years here in explaining the impact and Susie's continued journey of moving into the cave of learning, but will just let you consider that on your own.

This was just the first day of the rest of her life (and others like you and I) who were impacted by this throughout our entire school career.

Q: At the end of Day ONE, how many hands were still going up?

A: A few, maybe, let's say about 15-20%. These are the people, and you know them from your school experience as well as your work world experience; that will be in any/all conversations. They are the ones who won't be left out of anything, the talkers, and dominators even. Before we leave the end of the first day, picture the interaction between 3-4 kids and the teacher as the others have gone into their safe caves. That number (15-20%) has an amazing correlation to most all teams in our society's workplaces, adult classrooms, group meetings, etc. On most teams, sad to say, there is usually about 15-20% that do all the talking in meetings and within groups, along with the supervisor, manager, teacher, preacher, etc. The remaining ones made their way into their caves many years ago in school or in job experiences where this lesson was reinforced over and over again. The kid and many adults now think, —It's safe in here and I do not ever want to look stupid again.‖

No one is the bad guy here. This is not about bad people. Not the teacher, who was never taught this leadership stuff. Not the kids (people), who laughed instinctively and never stopped. Not the dominators in team meetings you work with now. Not the ones who knew the answer(s). Certainly the ones in the cave aren't bad people either although now they won't help with team decisions, problem solving, discussions, etc.).

This is just a story to help you think about this LEARNING principle. How have you been impacted?

*****

There are other societal factors and reasons that lead to this Non-LEARNER mentality, but we'll save that for another day. For now just suffice it to say, there are many reasons that have led our society and people to not be into learning, but rather to do anything possible to avoid being the stupid one.

As you move forward in this principle of learning, please realize that you and many, many, many others have good reason for not being good with this learning principle. So digest the reasons for why you are where you are, and STARTING NOW, change your thinking of the value of learning and growing. How about this - when you don't know something, 1) you ask, 2) you learn, 3) now you know more than you did. What a concept!

> *Remember back before the Day #1 question…
> When you still believed Learning was a good thing; well it still is!

Briefly, I just want to challenge you with a few more odds and ends about learning that may help in your focus on the Learner principle…

In every situation where you change roles - a new season begins. Beginning means you are new, you do not know everything; you have much to learn. Ask and pursue knowledge and wisdom.

People in roles of leadership, teaching, consulting, management, preaching or any position of perceived expertise – will struggle with this dynamic of learning. You see, when one achieves a level, position or title – naturally, a subconscious thought sets up in their minds. I know it all. I am the smartest one here. I know and they do not. They need my wisdom. I am here to tell them and share my smarts....' Avoid ever believing you are an expert (even if you are).

> ....this unconscious behavior does not make him/her a bad person. Although it *will* over time, in most cases - as they begin to struggle with the deeper meaning of what is going wrong here between leader and follower / teacher and student, expert and...etc.

Regarding God, Faith and well finding Jesus, consider this. When one is saved and comes to know God, we are beginning anew. We know hardly anything. We only know God, not His Teaching. Learning needs to begin. However, with so many, being saved becomes a mindset of now being in a position of knowing something others do not know, do not possess, etc. You see where that's going huh? It is how many Christians go afoul in various ways unknowingly. Remember, the very wording, being born again or saved implies new-ness, so stop talking and begin learning.

STORY... I have to tell you one of the neat lessons I picked up in life. I call it my **2LT**- (I am Sorry) lesson. Briefly, **2LT** is a Second Lieutenant in the Army; which I was, at one point in time. **2LT**s are the most junior officer level and partly, due to this, they are known to not know much, likely to make mistakes, etc. Well, at that time, I fitted in this mode quite well as a **2LT**. I could make mistakes as well as anyone, with the best of them!

> Here's the lesson I learned quickly (unlike many). I discovered that admitting to mistakes and apologizing was a good thing. On so many levels that kind of humbleness has such great benefits. I need not go on, but will just ask you – who do you know that struggles with not admitting mistakes, cannot ever be wrong, has to win, etc.? We're not thinking of you are we?

Apologizing
Does not always mean that you're wrong and the other person is right. It just means that you value your relationship more than your ego

---

I didn't mean to attack you, but I DID IT and I AM SORRY☺.

Can I also share with you that in all of my years of leadership work, that the unwillingness to admit mistakes is easily in the top 3 issues or complaints most have about their bosses? This is about leaders incapable of being wrong, having to have the right answer, things being done their way, etc.

This is not just about leaders however. This is about you and me and all of us knuckleheads. Learn to take responsibility, be okay with being wrong and learning from it, forget about excuses, just apologize and move on. A huge step toward significance.

Admitting mistakes and apologizing is so disarming to the one who found you out. Where does it leave them to go in this attack on you? Likely they will be shocked and have nothing else to say but oh and they also are ready to move on past the mistake. This is all a good thing.

*Can I urge you starting now to come out of your Safe Non-Learning Cave and begin learning again? Start now with questions that should have been asked previously in any/all parts of your life. BE a learner.

It is such a funny, ironic, sad and twisted thing that happens with so many of us knuckleheads regarding learning in new situations.

We don't ask questions because of the age-old dilemma that faces us all - we don't want to appear ignorant or ‗like we don't know'. And then later on, we don't ask because we are surely expected to know now! Are we knuckleheads or what?

*****

Some Odds n Ends or just good food for thought regarding LEARNING as well as some learning I have acquired:

    Failure is a good thing if and only if, we learned something from it!

    Try to develop critical thinking as you analyze decisions, vs. leaping mindlessly. Avoid ever having to say again, "It seemed like a good idea at the time... (Or) What was I thinking?

    Possess the mindset (even when you get good at something), that you will never get there ...there is always more to learn ...more to know ...there might be better ways.

    The current way is the unchanging old way now – think about that one ☺. This pertains to organizations, cultures, processes, and people. It is just a fact – if you are not changing, you cannot be learning, growing, and improving!

    Learn about the SLIGHT EDGE concept. It's not mine, but it is very real and a great mindset to possess. Go Google it, but basically in many ways it is just about always getting a little bit better. The best analogy I can come up with is one I read somewhere and is tied to the sport of baseball. Think of this...

> [A great hitter in baseball gets 3 hits out of every 10 times at bat. If he/she can do the little things well enough to just get one more hit every ten times up (4/10), he/she will be among the very best that ever played the game - a Hall of Famer for sure.
> There are other analogies, but you get it. Always be seeking a way to improve even a little bit. Think of doing this in your personal life. Think of a business that could get every employee to do this or even just some of them. LEARNING is all about possessing a learning mentality to give you a slight edge over 90% of people in this world.]

Two heads are better than one (implying that ten are even better). Sure you agree, but do you practice it in your interactions with others? Is doing it your way using the concept? How often do we make decisions all on our own? Think of the implications of this for someone in a leadership role, not using the team and those ten heads? Think of it as you and I try to do stuff without involving God?

If you believe something and nine others believe the opposite, you might want to listen... I'm just saying☺.

We all need to know what this is all about...

You CANNOT not
'LEAD BY EXAMPLE'!
(think about it...)

I would rather see a sermon
than hear one any day...

I'd rather you would walk with me,
than merely show the way...

The lectures you deliver
may be very wise and true,
but I think I'll get my lesson
by watching what you do...

Because I might misunderstand you,
and all the high advice you give,
but there's no misunderstanding
how you act and how you live.

We are ALWAYS
'LEADING BY EXAMPLE'

...we are ALWAYS marketing ourselves. Everything you say or do - the people you hang with, what you place on Facebook, etc. is telling your story. Learn this before you get forced to learn this.

When I was young, my father routinely shared this little keeper:

> **Don't ever do anything you don't want put in the newspaper, mentioned at church, or shouted in the halls at school.**

.

****

We ALL need help!' It's hard to argue with that, right? I realized something a few years back while in a season transition - looking & searching for so many things, - to include a job!

In conversations with a new friend and business acquaintance, this dynamic of 'seeking & accepting input from others' became so evident.

Boy did I need some help.

The bottom line is that we all need input, assistance, mentors, and coaches in our lives—ALL of us. I want to also share some thoughts regarding first impressions during that period of time for me personally.

Quite by chance, I stumbled into the path of someone who helped fill that mentoring void for me. It took some boldness on his part, but I received invaluable input, observations, and critiquing of ME. Some bad habits & behaviors had developed and needed to be addressed in presenting and marketing myself. As I was receiving this input, I had choices to make; 1) Would I get mad at _these things' I was hearing about ME, and 2) Should I defend and reject the input or thank this person for their input?

By the way, how do you respond to constructive criticism? For many people, hearing negative things about themselves typically ruins their day.

Our response should be THANK YOU!

Why thank the person giving constructive criticism? The answer is, because, this person has just HELPED you. For me, these observations back then were right on, hurt a bit – and were easily corrected.

I thought about how many people may have written me off or thought less of me because of those quirks (those initial impressions)? Why didn't THEY tell me right then and there? You and I know the answer: they didn't feel comfortable enough; the relationship wasn't strong enough or they didn't want to hurt my feelings, right?

You and I must have those people in our lives to help us, to point out the flaws we do not see. If you have no one like this, find someone! Seek out a mentor(s) who can help you before you go do one more interview, hit another networking event, or find yourself around other people you want to impress.

Do you really want to know? Don't ask others if you don't want to hear the negative as well as the positive. Please do realize that those who offer nothing for you to work on are useless to you – think about it.

Remember, you only get that one chance to make a first impression. Don't just depend on yourself to make that impression a good one. After all, we are a bit biased when it comes to us!

✳✳✳

STORY... (A favorite story of Learning)

After several years teaching about learning, problem solving, critical thinking, open-mindedness, assuming, etc. - this real life scenario played out about 3 years ago.

For many years, I had been thinking that '_when I became old ☺, I was going to smoke a pipe'. I had this notion that it would be cool to smoke a pipe, I would look distinguished, liked the smell, whatever. Besides the intrigue of all that and more, my Uncle Jack (deceased many years ago) had smoked a pipe. I loved him, he was cool and a distinguished older gentleman, and so, all the more reason for my decision.

OK, so a few years back when I was in my early 50's, I guess I had decided I was old enough, and began to tinker with smoking a pipe. I only did so outside, in the cold weather, throwing on the big coat, hat, scarf, and strolling around like a cool dude, profiling – doing the whole pipe thing.

I had a trip planned back home to see my parents and knew that when I pulled out the pipe, they were going to mess with me, call me a dummy, etc. We love each other very much, but this idea is stupid, so I knew I had the harassment due for smoking, even if it was a cool pipe. The time came, I put on the coat, hat, and headed to the back deck, lit up and here came the parents. As expected, the questioning began, harassment kicked in, the-you-crazy-idiot comments came forth and it was time to respond.

I begin to share my thinking and plans for many years, which do no good, so I pull out my ace (Uncle Jack). ―I know it's crazy, but blah, blah, blah and I so thought Uncle Jack was great and he smoked a pipe and...‖

I was cut off at the pass, being told that this piece of information, the fact in my head, my ace ―was indeed wrong. Uncle Jack never smoked a pipe I was told. ―What? Yes he did...uh, huh, you sure...‖

It hit me rather quickly (especially after having now taught several Critical Thinking courses) that I might just be wrong. After all logic said that my parents had lived with him many more years than I had. My arguing quickly subsided as I gave in reluctantly, to being possibly wrong.

My story here is no longer about smoking a pipe, me or bless his heart, my Uncle Jack. It is about the lessons learned for all of us about this story:

> Think about how tough it is being wrong when the opposition is not a friend, loved one, or good relationship.
>
> Consider your situations and worlds where it is may be difficult to admit mistakes, etc. How hard in a case like this, would it be for any of us to give up the fight and acknowledge we are wrong? The point here is whatever your role

(especially in maybe leader roles) ...builds the relationship strong!

How much in our (your) head(s) could be wrong?

Work with me here – some questions for you:

(?) Consider what percentage of stuff in your head is right or wrong.

(?) Where do we get the stuff in our heads (our brain)?

(?) Of the stuff in our heads, how much was actually critically evaluated before internalizing it into fact?
My informal research over couple of decades and with easily a few thousand people would suggest that between 45-60% could be in error. This, along with assumptions (that we don't even know we are making at times), suggest that we are frequently arguing from flawed information we have indeed taken in as fact!?!

> * FYI: Uncle Jack did smoke cigars, so I am not totally wrong. To be totally transparent, see how difficult it is to be wrong? If little stupid stuff like this is challenging, how challenging is it with stuff that really matters in life, work, and everywhere we journey?

*Let me leave you with this belief of mine after many years in the adult-learning and teaching profession – most of us are not really LEARNERS at heart. I think so many dynamics in life, not the least being a terribly ineffective education system in our country, leaves people without a desire to learn - or recognition of the value of learning.

Rather, most have somehow evolved into thinking life is all about being right and never being caught without an answer or being wrong. Learning mentalities are a rare commodity in people these days. Most do not have it.

Starting now, significantly try to develop an appreciation for learning new things. Nobody likes the always right kind of person. For sure God speaks harshly about foolish pride. As stated earlier, those incapable of accepting correction are stupid. That's in scripture!

**See everything.
Overlook a great deal.
Improve a little always.**
Pope John XXIII

DYSFUNCTIONAL **LEARNER** DYNAMICS

The non-learner stays the same, thinking the way I used to be is just fine'. I am not conforming/cutting my hair, wearing what they want me to wear, etc.....

Someone who is not significant in Learning thinks they know more, or are smarter than others.

This type of person is maybe one of the toughest types of people for me to love, to figure out, to help or get through to... He is that one that cannot be wrong. She will defend anything or say anything to keep from having to say she was wrong. It is insulting to them to have it suggested they were in err. Not knowing or making a mistake is embarrassing on some crazy self-esteem level.

Continuous Improvement is not understood by him/her, and is rarely even considered.

This person is insecure. If you know something, did something they didn't do, etc. – you pose as some sort of threat or opposition in their mind. They must prove somehow that he/she has also 'been there, done that'.

<u>Anyone or anything come to mind at this moment?</u>

Children Learn What They Live

If children live with criticism, they learn to <u>condemn</u>. If children live with hostility, they learn to <u>fight</u>.

If children live with fear, they learn to be <u>apprehensive</u>.
    If children live with pity, they learn to feel <u>sorry for themselves</u>.
If children live with ridicule, they learn to feel <u>shy</u>.
    If children live with jealousy, they learn
    to feel <u>envy</u>. If children live with shame,
    they learn to feel <u>guilty</u>.

If children live with encouragement, they learn confidence.

If children live with tolerance, they learn patience.
    If children live with praise, they learn appreciation.
    If children live with acceptance, they learn to love.
    If children live with approval, they learn to like
    themselves. If children live with recognition,
    they learn it is good to have a goal.

If children live with sharing, they learn generosity.
    If children live with honesty, they learn truthfulness.
    If children live with fairness, they learn justice.
    If children live with kindness and consideration,
    they learn respect.

If children live with security, they learn to have faith in themselves and in those about them.

*****

    If children live with friendliness, they learn the world
    is a nice place in which to live.

Copyright 1972 by Dorothy Law Nolte

...If any of these underlined (above) describe or fit you and who you are - realize you came by it honestly; someone taught you.

Significance starts now ...so begin UN-learning destructive behaviors, habits, or mindsets. For sure, whatever you do, do not pass them on!

I have come to believe that the key to:
Success ···Peace ···Happiness ···Significance & Leadership
Is a MIND & HEART that is

FOCUSED ON OTHERS

In my work in Adult Learning and Leadership, I re-packaged the above great piece of work, rewording / putting it this way:

EVERYTHING LEADERS NEED TO KNOW:

IF -We Live with Criticism…We Learn to Condemn.

IF -We Live with Hostility…We Learn to Fight.

IF -We Live with Ridicule…We Learn to be Shy.

IF -We Live with Shame…We Learn to feel Guilty.

IF -We Live with Tolerance…We Learn to be Patient.

IF -We Live with Praise…We Learn to Appreciate.

IF -We Live with Fairness…We Learn Justice.

IF -We Live with Approval…We Learn to Like Ourselves.

IF -We Live with Acceptance and Friendship…

…We find the World (and workplace) to be Good and Positive!

Some bonus thought for ya:

We wonder why people won't get involved-- when we know that most people really do care and want to be involved! Consider how we discourage risk-taking and why 'teamwork' doesn't seem to be working. Discouragement, poor attitudes, and low morale occur when we ridicule, ignore, and criticize for trying and failing, or never ask for their help...instead of encouraging & praising for the effort, and then coaching to ensure that we all learn from our failures.

Here is the challenge for organizations: Many leaders and managers in our organizations did not necessarily live and learn from a good model regarding the treatment (and leading) of people. Therefore, organizations have a very high likelihood of the wrong 'stuff' being modeled, unless we very clearly address the right principles and values through our people-development processes. Should we just leave this all to chance knowing today's family and societal dynamics??!

LOVE MEANS
THAT YOU
ACCEPT A PERSON
WITH ALL THEIR
**FAILURES,
STUPIDITIES,
UGLY POINTS,**
AND NONETHELESS, YOU SEE
PERFECTION
IN
IMPERFECTION ITSELF.

SIGNIFICANT QUESTIONS ON LEARNING:

1. Is it difficult for you to be wrong?

2. Do you feel yourself needing to win, when in discussions?

3. Are you open to other's ideas?
4. Do you tend to view things as a single event or part of a process?

5. Is CHANGE a challenging concept to you?

6. Are you a teacher with others in your world(s)?

7. When was the last season of your life when you really felt you had grown?

8. Are there challenges coming up that will require you learning, growing, changing, and possibly discovering more about you?

9. How do you view the concept of Continuous Improvement; is it part of your professional and/or personal life?

10. What could you learn more about right now in your life that would benefit you clearly?

11. How do you deal with others who are closed minded, stuck on themselves always needing to be right, etc.?

12. Are you an effective brain-stormer / out of the box thinker?

13. When you come up against something you don't know about, do you tend to embrace learning about it or avoid it?

14. What kind of environment or situation do you need to be in a learning mode personally?

15. Do you seek out new experiences; new people?

*As you considered many of these questions, did you think of them in all worlds – at work and at home as well?

*If you are a Learner and want more from the perspective of Leadership-Learning, please let me know. My first book was about a most significant leadership/teaching concept I call Teaching Fishing

…Give a Man a Fish and he eats today; Teach Him to Fish and he eats for a Lifetime.

Please consider getting the book, it is a short, easy read and if you like I will ship you the eBook for free. Look for the title 'TEACHING FISHING LEADERSHIP'.

I would be happy to send you a **FREE** eBook version...

www.bookertraining.com/2.html

One last thing, I promise, before we leave the topic of LEARNING. The following is an excerpt from my third book on Leadership – The Conference for Leaders'.

It is an opening talk at a Leadership Conference where the conference host is challenging the audience to learn...

"...take a look at this box that I am putting up on the screen. I'll only show it to you for a moment. It's a box with a hole in it. Quickly examine the picture and decide which surface the hole is in?"

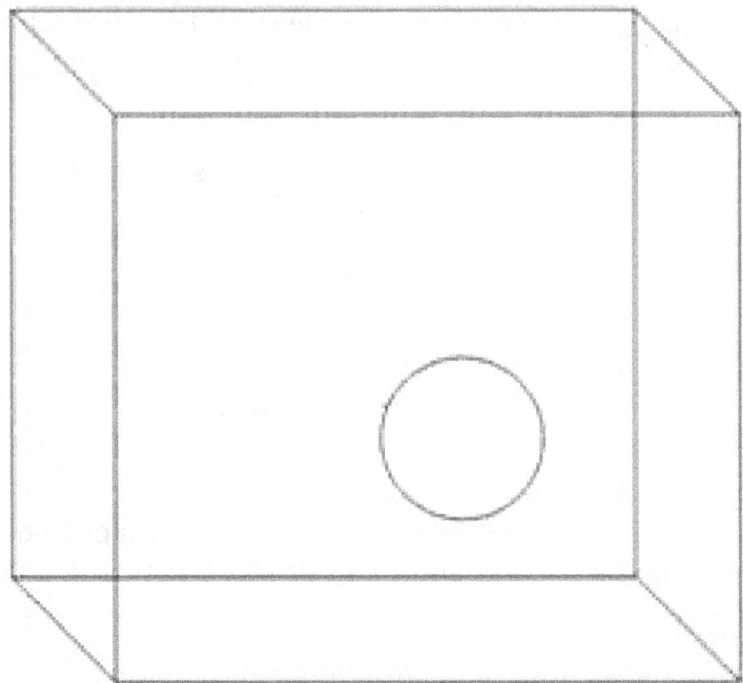

I allowed the participants a few seconds to view the slide, and then clicked to a blank screen. I then asked ...So, where did you see the hole?

...How many think the hole is in the front of the cube, in the lower right-hand corner? I asked, and several hands were raised. ...How many think it's in the front of the cube, somewhere towards the center? I asked and other hands were raised. ...How many think it's in the back somewhere? I asked, and still other participants raised their hands. ...Okay, I said.

...Now, look againll and I projected the slide for a few more seconds. This time, did you notice that the hole was somewhere...different?

Lots of hands were raised, as people in the audience realized that they could not only see the hole on the first surface they saw it on, but on two or three other surfaces, as well. ...Okay look one last time I said, and turned the slide back on for good. I asked the participants to visualize the hole on every possible surface, front center, front lower right, back surface lower right, in the top surface looking down, and so on.

...Here's another thought, maybe it's just a ball floating, and there's no hole at all! Everyone laughed, and some people talked amongst themselves and pointed. Some people even argued with each other about what surface the hole was on and whether it was a hole or a floating ball. I regained their attention. ...What does all this mean? What's the point here? I asked as he strolled up and down the stage, taking a few responses from the audience. He continued ....All those interpretations you suggested are correct.

This is an exercise that encourages seeing things from a different perspective with an open mind. However, the main lesson in looking at this box is what you just experienced. After seeing it in one or maybe two places initially, you were eventually able to see it in four, five, or even six possible places. Think about this, now—why were you able to? What enabled you to see other possibilities?

I paused and listened to a few responses that were shouted out and then went on to answer the own question.

...It's because you were *willing* to try to see a different perspective!

How often is this lack of perspective or open-mindedness a problem for you, your boss, your team, and everyone else around you? You get it, right? This has everything to do with conflict, relationships, agreement, consensus, contemplation, and involving others, as well as other dynamics that we'll be hitting on here over the weekend.

...If you showed up skeptical, are you willing to see the hole in other places? Are you willing to see things beyond your current thinking? Are you open to the different perspectives you'll encounter here over the next two days? If so, we hope you will carry this open-mindedness with you as you go through the first breakout session, and the other sessions, too. I am confident that you will see great benefits if you do, and see some things from perspectives you hadn't considered before...

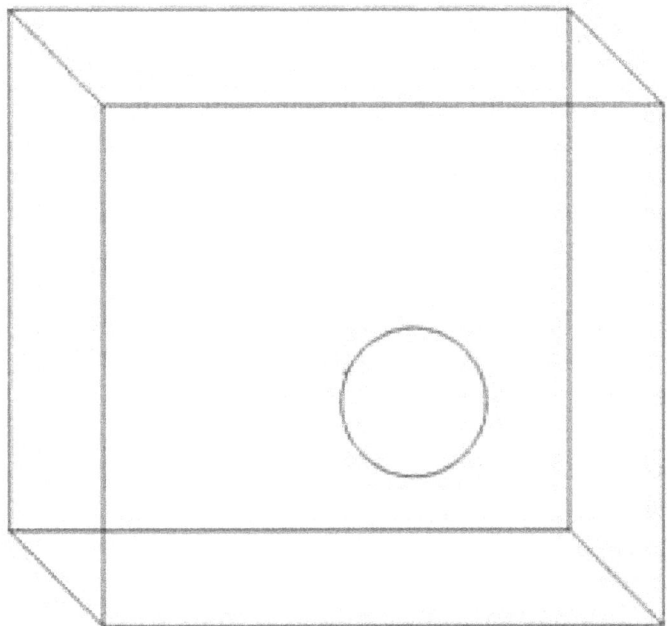

INTERMISSION (begins)

I placed this right smack in the middle of this book, for a variety of reasons; the reasons do not much matter the point here does. Likely, the primary reason is because for some, I wanted you hooked before dropping this on you.

Here's the deal as I see it – how you live matters. What it guarantees you is nothing. Living right and significantly is still the right thing to do. Let me ramble a moment.

Very likely you have already touched on this point in your reading and thinking. You, a friend, or some person in your life, lives a life of significance and bad things have occurred to them. Here is this seemingly great person, maybe even seemingly perfect person you know, that has just discovered they have cancer. We all know people (again realizing we may be talking about you here) who fall into that category of bad things happen to good people.

This is tough stuff to accept and handle. You may or may not believe in God, but even if you do not, you have likely challenged God on this topic. How God ...your God, let this happen to her? How could a God of Mercy and Love allow all those people to...? You know the stories and so do I.

I will tell you right here, these are questions of God I also do not understand. I have come to believe and trust (although just like anyone, I have this belief challenged some at times) that God does things in ways we just cannot understand.

Can I tell you here that I DO understand that? I do and can understand that God being the God that He is, having created all this, has a plan, and His ways I cannot fathom. This makes perfect sense to me. How could I possibly understand the big picture of how ALL THIS works. The zillion years of time, the zillion people who lived and do live, the good and the bad that occurs, the connections that happen, nature, life, death, eternity, ...and ALL THAT.

I get that I don't get to understand that. I am okay with that. That makes sense☺.

As it was my intention, I did write this book to try to convince anyone about God – I will not try here either. Whether you believe or not, how you live your life matters.

You have read this far, and so I have to believe that it is important to you, being Significant in your walk, your life, and when you go away.
On some level, for some reason, this is important to you.

Because of this, I thought it only made sense to touch on this. We deserve nothing. We are owed nothing. We are guaranteed nothing. If you Believe in God, then that is something for you and God to sort out.
If you do not believe in God, then who is it that owes you anything I have to wonder? Other people ...the world ...the government, etc.?

Good stuff has happened to good people since the world began, I am sure. It is happening now, it has in my past and I am positive it will continue to be that way.

As this book has been about YOU up till now, it remains about you, and will finish that way – it is about YOU and your significance. Do you care to be significant? Do you need a reason for caring?

INTERMISSION

(Over)

TRANSPARENCY

…Being real is what everyone wants in others. Being un-real is the way most live their lives. Knowing the person through a trusting, open and real relationship is when truly effective communication happens.
Being who you really are is leading a life of significance, truth and fruitfulness. Pride once again negatively impacts this principle - being something other than which you really are.
Nobody believes it; everyone knows you are not perfect; become okay with being the flawed one you really are. Unconditional acceptance, friendship and love only evolve when we are transparent with the other.
At work, play or anywhere in between - anything good between two people <u>requires transparency</u>.

Transparency is a characteristic, principle, and trait that has drawn my attention in recent years in my work with people and leadership. I see transparency as such an important dynamic related very closely to trust, real relationships, and in general, any productive relationship must include transparency between two or more people. We are all naturally inclined to BE non-transparent I believe.

I read somewhere recently some interesting words about this, approaching it from the standpoint of meekness. Regarding this issue, consider this paraphrasing from some writings of A.W.Tozer…

…that we deal with so much internal inward poverty – we doctor up impressions we put out there for others; we artificially present ourselves; we are all so in need of deliverance from pretense in how we live…

The Word says that we should become as little children, who, early on have not developed all this internal strife in comparing ourselves to others, etc. Our landscape these days has changed with so many people interacting with others online through social networking. In one sense, I see people more than ever, putting up this sort of façade in face to face relationships. People try to convince others all is good, they are on top of the world, blah, blah, blah. On the other hand, many leap onto Facebook and spill their guts about how they feel, their issues with Him, their boss being the worst animal in the world; mom is a pain, blah, blah, blah. Talking about transparency done the wrong way!?! *tip from the coach, every company these days, will go to your online profiles, and that becomes indirectly part of the interview process. As we begin to post something on those networks, ask yourself if this is something that might damage me if read by someone not intended.

This is not how transparency serves us best. Transparency as I am speaking to here is about the openness and real-ness between two real people anywhere and everywhere. It is the intimacy of real and meaningful relationships.

This is not just about love in a romantic sense with a significant other, but any meaningful relationship desired in life – two friends, coworkers, buddies, business owner and a customer, parent and child, ...you and anyone!

*To be transparent has its risks. It is allowing people to know who you really are; displaying that 90% of the iceberg part! It is allowing people to see who you really are; know who you really are; understand what you really think – including your flaws.

I can tell you right now, without any doubt; the only solid relationships in life, those really good ones, are the ones where the Principle of Transparency is alive and well between the two of you.

What does this suggest of the others in life? Lies and deceit sound harsh, but they are in reality a non-transparent person is about.

People believe you to be fine, and you are not. People think you are rich, and you are nearing bankruptcy. People think you can handle it, when you cannot.

*****

Get it? Why do we do this? Why do you and I do this?

Go back to that one person in your life that you are real with; what is so good about it? I'll bet I know – EVERYTHING! Trust, support, better ideas, comfort, peace, fruitfulness, forgiveness, and thanks are all part of it. It works. It is the only worthwhile relationship you seek out day in and day out; when you get a chance it is who you want to be with, right?

Significance, in any sense, can only come from reality, from you being precisely who you are.

Do you want others to see what you are about? Do you want others to know your principles, values, and beliefs? Consider this – are we lying if we are not transparent?

Any relationship that is not what it ought to be is likely because one or both of the parties are not being transparent.

When a relationship is good, right, and true, we KNOW that person; they KNOW us. Why can we not understand this as humans ...and as leaders?

"How are you?"

Broken. Useless. Alone. Clueless. Confused. Betrayed. Fragile. On the verge of tears. Depressed. Anxious. About to break down. Ready to give up. Pathetic. Annoying. I'm just a burden. Distant. Lonely. Bitter. Heartbroken. Lovely. Rejected. Crushed. I feel like I'm going to just fall apart at any moment. Empty. Defeated. Never good enough.

Fine.

When I am real; when I share my concerns, flaws, weaknesses, and issues - I have strengthened our relationship (not weakened it, as some unknowing people/managers like to believe). Can I be wrong with this person without having to throw up a defensive wall; can they know I am imperfect and sometimes I may make a mistake?

...now, that's transparency; that's real and that's who you are.

*****

Instead, people (of course this is not about you and me☺) tend to be prideful, be someone we are not, put on airs, act as if everything is fine, what you did or said did not bother me... I have no problems; it is all good; I better not let you in, because you might learn I have flaws...issues, etc. You are perfect, never make mistakes, and cannot admit you were wrong... If they know that about me, they won't like me...

*You know it strikes me here that if someone doesn't like you because they found out something about you, discovered a mistake you made or otherwise you let them in on who you really are – you do not need that person in your close transparent world.

I would just challenge you to consider the people in your life where the relationship is truly meaningful. What makes them or that relationship meaningful? I will just say this – if it is significant and meaningful, transparency is alive and well between you.

BE TRANSPARENT IN ALL YOU ARE & BELIEVE

I struggled with transparency in my faith in God, & Jesus (see that was good and transparent – I shared that with you ☺) It has been a bit of a challenge in letting that be part of who I am wherever I am, and always...

I will tell you that the struggle has paid huge dividends in new, quality people in my life, business opportunities, etc. Coming out of the Closet as I term it, has been nothing but good; I mean nothing but good. I am sure that transparency has led some to distance themselves from me – although I could not tell you any one person that I know that of for sure. Again, here's the deal: If they (whoever they are) choose to disconnect after discovering something previously unknown about you and who you are – they needed to go away. I would even say that Continuous Improvement is happening in your life. You have now lost a judgmental, closed-minded person from your world – that was not a real friend or relationship. Make sense?

Is it too late to become transparent in some relationships in our lives?

For me, in my new relationships from now on, I intend to try and be more transparent from the beginning. How about you?

BE TRANSPARENT BEFORE IT IS TOO LATE

Transparency is such a huge dynamic in my life right now. Everyone experiences sooner or later loved ones passing away from this life. I have been fairly lucky in this regard until recently; as I have now lost three very significant people from my world. Undoubtedly one of the toughest things we human beings deal with is losing loved ones.

Can I tell you something that has rung so true with me; I am going to anyway. Tell people how much they mean to you, how much you love them and their importance to your world – before it is too late. I believe this happens with people all the time, not accomplishing this. This totally ties into the principle of FORGIVENESS now doesn't it? I urge you to make things right, before something happens and you cannot correct it.

Be transparent for Work, Home, and All Relationships. The rewards far outweigh the risks!

TRUST

The knowledge that you will not deliberately or consciously take unfair advantage of me. That I can put my situation, problems, opinions and self-esteem in your hands with confidence.

Loyalty to each other is highly valued and is a top priority to each of us.

EVEN AFTER YOU HAVE BEEN BURNED

People will likely break your trust again in the future. Are you going to let them cause you to be an un-trusting, stereotyping and nontransparent person?

STORY...   Here's a real story I have shared many times that taught me a lesson or two. I was a **1LT** and Platoon Leader in an Army Infantry organization in the beginning years of my season in the military. I had a very good soldier who I counted on, trusted, and would have actually considered being one of my top 2 or 3 soldiers.

A situation arose and Specialist Walton we will call Him, was accused of some connection with drugs. I do not remember any other details - just that the accusation was drug related and could not be true. You think you know where this is headed huh?

I looked this best soldier of mine, my trusted friend, in the eyes and asked Him about the accusations. He denied the whole thing. Enough said as far as I was concerned, he didn't do it and I was going to bat for Him. To make a long story short, he did it. After some further discussions and investigation, he was finally caught and even confessed.

Now here's the message for all of us here. Don't let the single incidents and situations in life turn you against the rest of the people in the world. You know that person (friend, family or foe) that lied and betrayed you; that was Him/her, not everyone else. Do not now let that one person make you into a distrusting individual who won't let others into your life.

It is likely that experience made a huge impact on me at the time and for some time thereafter. Likely it still has some significance in my trust and transparency principle even today. Fortunately working in the field I do, I was able to put that behind me. Very likely my work with leadership, people stuff, trust, and relationships led me to realize that I need to not let that impact me further.

*****

It's funny, as I just got a visual image of a transparent plastic sheet of stuff and how you look right through it – like plastic wrap or something. That's transparency; seeing through it, nothing hidden. Is that you, can people see right through you, even predict your motives and actions, is that okay? Is that a good or bad thing from your perspective? It kind of puts a whole new spin on that old phrase of not being thin-skinned or not letting him/her get under your skin!

Do not be superficial, be candid, share your thoughts, feelings, opinions, mistakes, sins, etc. Can we be too clear? It strikes me that transparency keeps people from being surprised by your actions.

Be Transparent all you Leaders!

Leaders (whether you are one now or in the future): please know that no one really believes you are this studly, perfect, not needing any help; possess no problems, you are all-knowing / master of all, with everything in life being awesome.

Be real with people and they will be real with you. There was after all only one Perfect One, and I for one know that it is not you. How about considering this the next time you take over a leadership role, from the start?

What if you are a leader and people do not know what you are about, how you think what your values, etc.? Following a leader that is not transparent is a guessing game that leaves people unknowing, worrying needlessly, always seeking a solution, etc. Be predictable! That means they know you and you know them. That's a good thing.

Everything just mentioned is a significant relationship description on any level; whether a leader or not.

EVEN WITH YOUR FLAWS & IMPERFECTIONS

Life and our culture has undoubtedly led us to be insecure; to believe that you should never be wrong; hide your imperfections and flaws, and never let *them* know your weaknesses.

This is just not true and you can accept it now or wait and learn it later in life. Any significant person or significant relationship in life will only occur with the security that you know that person(s) and vice versa.

✳✳✳

BE TRANSPARENT IN WHAT GOD TELLS YA... (Or did HE really)!

You may not like this, but I am going to say it regardless. I believe great, significant people of faith do not realize the harm they may be doing in how they are communicating their belief with others. This is about carelessly telling others how God told you this or that.

Now I do not discount or disbelieve that God speaks to people. I will tell you I have never really heard Him directly, audibly. I am okay with that assuming and guessing God likely has plenty of stuff to do☺).

My point here is best made by relating back to days before I knew Jesus, my God and become new. I can remember my skeptical thinking when someone would tell me something like God told me this or that... Again, I can believe that God speaks to people directly; when I hear it now, I can accept that. I do however believe there are plenty who just say it as part of an unconscious communication of their thoughts and feelings. Carelessly spouting this with no wrong intent may negatively be impacting some who hear and are confused.

How often do we hear people recount things said and the next day we hear, 'I guess He didn't say that, mean that...' or some such comment. Now, being a skeptic at that time, I am sure I thought that was a lie, God didn't really talk to him/her to begin with, I knew that.

Remember, our topic here and focus is on Transparency. All I am saying and suggesting for all of us of faith is – be real, honest, and truthful. The other person doesn't know you really meant to say I THINK God is telling me to...

That may seem unimportant but that qualifier is huge to your transparency, real-ness, trustworthiness, and maybe even leading someone to the Lord (or not).

DYSFUNCTIONAL TRANSPARENCY DYNAMICS

Being too transparent *could* be an issue - wearing out people with YOUR problems, issues, complaints, and truths. However, here's the deal with this: if it was truly a transparent relationship, he/she would be telling you (that you are dumping too much on them)! Instead, likely for lack of relationship (and transparency) between you and others, they are telling other people instead of you.

Something about all this reminds me of that cool leadership quote:

…Effective leaders realize they must get the heart before asking for the Hand,
anonymous

I connect this with the above, in that, when we get to the heart in a relationship, we can ask for a hand or lend a hand in help (with their problems, issues, complaints, etc. from above ☺).

In order for transparency to be there must be give and take; both sides have to want to go there. It is only when we truly achieve transparency with another, we discover, and uncover boundaries in areas between you. Boundaries are a good thing and that fine line of transparency is where we grow and really connect.

> A lack of transparency is seen, defined, and recognized by: shallow, superficial comments and understanding of each other never moving beyond where we are right now telling other people (rather than the person) of their imperfections.
> Misunderstanding and assumptions on a myriad of levels.

> **Anyone or anything come to mind at this moment:**

SIGNIFICANT QUESTIONS ON TRANSPARENCY:

1. Do people really know who you are?

2. Do you allow others into your world; maybe just your closest friends?

3. Would it help your world(s) in any way, if people knew more about you?

4. Do you trust people until they betray you; or do you not trust people until they earn it?

5. Where (and who) is a lack of Transparency effecting the growth of a relationship in your life?

6. How do you see TRUST relating to the principle of TRANSPARENCY?

7. What prevents people from being transparent with other people?

8. What do you believe people think about you and who you are, what you are about, etc.?

9. Are there any advantages to a person being transparent?

10. Can or should a leader be transparent; how about a follower/employee?

11. Are you predictable in the important stuff, like values?

12. Do you say what you mean or what you think you should say (do)?

13. Did you really hear Him?

14. Do you put on a show for others?

15. Do you have some screwed up perception of how people should act or are you comfortable enough to just BE who you really are?

THANKFUL

…One need only to open her eyes for a moment and (pause in dwelling on her own problems), then to look around anywhere and see the struggles, pain and troubles of so many! That instant feeling arising in you and any of us, is thankfulness and appreciation that you do not have their troubles. Thankfulness comes only from once again taking the focus from self and onto others; then we see how good we have it. The significantly-thankful individual knows we deserve nothing more than we have at any moment. Give thanks and be thankful daily and even before you receive…

    I think the truly significant person practices Thankfulness by giving thanks before receiving something. This person has the heart of appreciating the moment in time, and everything that has been given to them.

IT DOESN'T GET ANY BETTER THAN THIS…

The phrase above, made popular years ago, had a message to it I really connected to for a while. There was a season of my life when I used it with everyone I encountered. It was MY greeting to anyone and everyone back then.

I used it for several years. I used it as an optimistic point of view to internalize and portray a positive attitude. As I think of it now in the context of thankfulness, I realize that was the primary message I was intending to portray to others. I was so thankful for being so blessed and all that I had.

Interestingly, it was during a time of some fairly challenging life struggles, and I think it helped me. It helped me maintain a perspective that life could be a whole lot more difficult.

It was also before I knew God. Somewhere in the midst of some deeper human struggles in life my, usage of the phrase slipped out my vocabulary.

In church recently, I began thinking about this old slogan for some strange reason. God, my pastors, our Sunday school class, and my church in general do that frequently (make me think). That is something I am very thankful for - that is a good thing in my book – THINKING.

I was praying for my wife's health, my work and business, finances, and oh yeah ...ALL those zillions of people in this world who are struggling with sooooo much more than I am!

It was in that moment of prayer, when that old phrase hit me. I was thinking of how - now so many years later, - now that I have BECOME NEW and God is all over my life, - now I should REALLY be using that phrase!

You see, life cannot be any better, because it is His Will and HE is there with me (and with us) huh?

Our struggles are relative, and someone is always worse off than we are. This doesn't diminish my issues; our struggles are completely real! It is where we are - the pains, suffering, and struggles are ours indeed. That place, this moment in time where we are currently, is as good as it gets, because He determines it so. If we trust in God, we can find peace even in the midst of turmoil. Give thanks daily.

We are to BE glad for this day - to be thankful for where we are, right?
Did this make any sense to you? Be thankful if it did☺!
   When good things happen, are you thankful? What is good at the moment for which you haven't expressed your thanks? No time like the present...?

'The Law of the Garbage Truck.'

This is something I came across recently, thought it was worth inserting here for your reading pleasure:

'The Law of the Garbage Truck.'

A gentleman was in a taxi. Suddenly a garbage truck came barreling through an intersection cutting off the cabbie and in making a sharp turn some trash actually fell onto the hood of the taxi. The gentleman was astonished observing the taxi cab driver wave to the truck heading on down the road, quietly saying, "No problem, stuff happens". The gentleman inquired why the driver did that and didn't go get Him; why he wasn't mad, etc.?
The cab driver reflected in pause for a moment and then explained that many people are like garbage trucks.
They run around full of garbage, full of frustration, full of anger, and full of disappointment. As their garbage piles up, they need a place to dump it and sometimes they'll dump it on you. Don't take it personally. Just smile, wave, wish them well,

and move on. Don't take their garbage and spread it to other people at work, at home, or on the streets. The bottom line is that successful people do not let garbage trucks take over their day. Life's too short to wake up in the morning with regrets, so ... Love the people who treat you right.
Pray for the ones who don't.
Life is ten percent what you make it and ninety percent how you take it!
Have a garbage-free day!

[And I will add ...and be thankful]

The principle of Thankfulness is much like our principle of Forgiveness. When you possess and practice these principles, life becomes so much more happy, peaceful, and _significant'. You are a better person, life becomes better, and people will be thankful to have you in their world. You will see things clearer.

When we do not understand and have not learned to appreciate, we will be miserable, lack peace big time, and friends will be in short supply. This is a fact. No one enjoys being around a person who is not thankful.

*Find a way to develop the habit of giving thanks for every little thing you have, stuff that happens to you, people in your life, etc. Remember as stated in James 1, which was already given to you earlier in this book, but a great fit here as well. Be thankful you get to think about it again☺.

...Consider it pure joy, my brothers and sisters, whenever you face trials of many kinds, because you know that the testing of your faith produces

perseverance. Let perseverance finish its work so that you may be mature and complete, not lacking anything. James 1:2

So if you can appreciate the trials, the struggles, and persevere through them with the, -It doesn't get any better than this attitude – you have acquired a thankful heart and mind. Are you there yet?

Right now, I am thankful for the moment and my personal relationship with my absolutely no#1 best friend, Jesus Christ. I am also thankful for a few of my friends who are going to share some further thoughts on the Principle of Thankfulness.

Through Jesus, therefore, let us continually offer to God a sacrifice of praise—the fruit of lips that openly profess his name. And do not forget to do good and to share with others, for with such sacrifices God is pleased.
Hebrews 13: 15-16

DYSFUNCTIONAL THANKFUL DYNAMICS

Victimization is one of the factors or behaviors indicating a lack of this principle of Thankfulness. It is about all the -bad stuff happens to me- thinking, bellyaching, and sharing with others of his/her woes.

Thankfulness is voided out by a mentality and thinking that you deserve better or that someone(s) owes you.

Without going into depth here on this issue; I will mention that it might just be represented by someone on welfare, food stamps, and every other form of subsistence given in this world. Please know that I am not criticizing you or anyone else who is in this world in need...

If you, or others you know, use the system in a taking mode with the -I deserve this- mentality then they do not fit in this discussion.

[BTW - IF THE SHOE DOESN'T FIT HERE, DON'T WEAR IT.]

Again, the point is made for those who need to hear this, do not fall into the trap of deservedness and forget about thankfulness. Enough said, I will assume, point made...?

Other indicators that come to mind:

>Complainer

>Taker vs. giver

>Selfish

>What else could someone do for me mentality

>Victim-mentality

>Rather receive than give

> **Anyone or anything come to mind at this moment:**

SIGNIFICANT QUESTIONS ON THANKFUL:

1. Who was the last person you forgot to thank?

2. Can you remember a time when you did something for someone and they failed to thank YOU? (Have you forgiven them, see Chap 2!)

3. How do you know if someone is thankful?

4. Do you appear thankful and appreciative to others?

5. What does God expect from us in terms of THANKFULNESS?

6. Can you think of people around you who are good/bad at this?

7. Have you ever witnessed, taught or mentored someone about this topic?

8. Do you take stuff for granted?

9. Do you appreciate what you have?

10. Who taught you (or didn't teach you☹) about being thankful?

11. Did you ever have someone hold a door for you and did you thank them?

12. Is thanking others and giving thanks instinctively you?

13. Who is the most thankful person you know; can something be learned from them? [Have you told them you admire this about them/why not?]

14. Would others view you as having a thankful personality or way about you?

15. Who owes you thanks?

LOVE -RELATIONSHIP

We are to love our brother, no matter what.
As the Word tells us, it is easy to love your brother, friends, and loved ones, even insignificant people do that! We are all made in God's image and therefore expected to accept and unconditionally love one another. Wow, do so many have this messed up in life. Do you truly like, enjoy, love and appreciate people.
So much is wrong in all of our worlds for lack of a trusting, real relationship. Grow current relations and find new relationships in life always. Love is what makes the world go round and is indeed the key to a happy, peaceful and productive life.
Communication problems are never really the issue, the Relationship is! Go fix a relationship in your life today and keep them always fruitful…

I learned it at home; everyone doesn't…

My parents taught me love. They showed me love - I was fortunate. I now realize that many and maybe most reading this may not have had the love of parents in their nurturing days.

This is a serious detriment and drain on our society these days, as so many have come from unloving situations in life. This is epidemic and contagious in the way people exist and function with each other. So many are seeking what they have never known, but because of how we were created, we crave and seek it – love and relationship.

It is also why I see God as such a huge factor in my life, which I hope I can introduce others here and along my journey. God does not disappoint and His love is real, never-ending, and unconditional. To really learn love on a level we have never known, we must somehow find our way to Jesus, our Lord, and God.

*I have learned so much from my profession working with people, culture, human behavior and organizations. An interesting discussion frequently occurs in my work with leaders, managers, supervisors, etc.... regarding the challenge and struggles of people working with other people. Specifically, not all others, just those few that make it difficult. You know the ones I'm referring to – those others!

We all have *those* people that we effectively relate to, like, trust, enjoy, and communicate well with...? Don't we also have those " *others*" , that don't quite live up to our expectations or just can't do enough _good things' to make us *like* them? They are different and rub you the wrong way somehow.

What is needed for any highly successful team or any relationship between two people is <u>unconditional</u> acceptance of one another! This is the kind of love and relationship we are supposed to have with others. We are to love God and all those He created (in His image by the way).

We all know that this is easier said than done. The more likely handling of these people is one of –...I need you to prove yourself, you need to change, your sins and flaws are unacceptable to me...‖   I believe our very nature of acceptance of each other is tied to their ability to live up to other's expectations. We have this way about us that (going back to the Transparency principle) causes us to be in turmoil; judging and critiquing everyone in comparison to ourselves. This is just not how we are supposed to be if we are to be living significantly.

We are all just not the same in our thoughts, actions, habits, ethics, logic, common sense level, etc....so we struggle, fight, or just avoid each other.

The only solution is hard, persistent work between people to maintain an agreement to unconditional acceptance, but also to agree to alert each other of when we do things that tug at this acceptance. This is not to mean that we should not have expectations of each other...or be accountable to each other.

For if you love those who love you, what reward do you have? Do not even the tax collectors do the same? Mat 5:46

It is not just a good thing to do or the right thing to do – it is practical and in your best interests to build bridges and relationships constantly. Do your best to keep them strong and never-ending. You just never know...

As we spoke to earlier, love and relationships are challenged at this point in time: The family dynamic is so broken and technology interferes with person to person interactions – we are not getting closer, but further away from each other. Sure we can communicate instantly with a person in China, but can you relate to the neighbor living 75 feet away?

Seek people out. Make yourself interact. Learn to love everyone. Do NOT let what is happening in this world, happen to you. Those that know how to love, and love even those *others* – WIN! They will be significant.

Love is patient, love is kind. It does not envy, it does not boast, it is not proud. It does not dishonor others, it is not self-seeking, it is not easily angered, and it keeps no record of wrongs. Love does not delight in evil but rejoices with the truth. It always protects, always trusts, always hopes, and always perseveres.

LOVE and liking people

Significance comes down to this – loving others. It is about an appreciation, general ‗liking', and love for mankind. It is about accepting others as you and placing them above yourself. He, she, or they are God's creation and we are to love them as we do the Lord. You can buy into the -God thing- here or not, but the substantive, successful, significant person will love people. People will know this about you.

STORY... Rodney, the Manager. I have to share with you a not so-funny story about this manager I met in my first few years in Leadership Development consulting. I was in Jonesboro, Arkansas, working with a small company and about eight leaders. We were in maybe our 8-10th hour of working on leadership, when Rodney interrupts with, ―Booker, I think I just figured out why I don't really enjoy supervising‖ . My non-verbal gestures encouraged Him to go on, which he did in remarking, ―I don't really like people. I assured Rodney that he was clearly onto something here (sarcastically shared I am sure). Rodney was a mess of a dude, totally entrenched in a way of carrying Himself, and conveying that he knew it all – about nearly everything. Rodney was not a loveable guy.

I share this with you, to emphasize and make you question yourself, do you like people, much less love them?

*I am sure Rodney came from dysfunction; there is hardly any other possible explanation. Alluding back to earlier discussions, this is one of the reasons for our book here – to create a framework and base for what so many in this world never really learned. We must love others.

> NO MATTER HOW EDUCATED, TALENTED, RICH, OR COOL YOU BELIEVE YOU ARE, HOW YOU TREAT PEOPLE ULTIMATELY TELLS ALL. INTEGRITY IS EVERYTHING

The Power of Relationships

Relationship(s) is what will make up your life – the good, the bad, and the ugly. Without relationships, we are useless. No man is an island. Let me share a recent story that exemplifies the importance of establishing, growing, and maintaining relationships. I know plenty of people who have similar stories, so please get the point here. Make them and keep them – relationships with all kinds of people. You never know what might happen with someone, that ugly duckling dynamic maybe plays out here.

Now sure, establish relationships with quality people that you hope will help your world. However, establish and keep them whether or not you see their value to you; focus on how you might add value to them first. It has to be this way with everything – your heart must be in the right place. Love people and develop relations with as many of those people in life as you can.

STORY...   Julie was a VP when I met her several years back. With management-development needs, she brought me in to consult with her (and her leadership team). We did lots of good work together, and after a few years, the work for various reasons ceased. We still had a good relationship, but things had run their course, and the consulting ended. Although we maintained contact for a while afterward, somehow we lost contact. I still included her in my blogs and email blasts, but was she receiving them? – I did not know.

Jumping forward 5 years, we re-connected and met for coffee this past summer. It was first and foremost such a great feeling to have my old friend part of my life again. We caught up on everything, and she told me of serious health issues that had occurred. A couple of very hard years of dealing with many surgeries, etc. ... She was now well and ready to go back to work. She had found work and she was (is) so excited about the position and opportunity; maybe more excited about how it came to pass. It was a relationship with a friend she had maintained; someone she had worked with for some number of years and who she had kept in touch with... This friend was now the corporate HR person for a very large company you know. This relationship had led to her being offered this amazing opportunity.

This story is about two situations and relationships bearing fruit after extended periods. First, Julie's life, and now mine, as Julie is bringing me back in to help with her new team!

You never know when a relationship will bear fruit; make it meaningful to the both of you. Keep growing the vine(s)!

Recently, I have become hugely interested in the relationships & parallels of my faith and the dynamics of leadership & relationships. A revelation hit me yesterday listening to a radio talk show. I hope you find something useful and relevant here. Either way, I always welcome your reactions, thinking, argument, etc.!

I frequently share with leaders in coaching, consulting or in academic management courses, about the value of establishing relationship(s) quickly and early on - before you need someone. As the new one (whether manager or employee), it just makes sense that while you are learning the ropes of the company and business, what better time to be making strong relationships? The fact is, we will NEED something from them; be ASKING for something; want their HELP; or be in CONFLICT with them sooner or later!

This is why it is so critical to have a relationship BEFORE you need them, right? Doesn't that make sense? Yet, so often people just start functioning around someone, or manage them without focusing on IT until IT is the problem – the undeveloped relationship!

STORY... It struck me listening to this Christian talk show and driving down the road how ludicrous this is, that we do this. I was trying to think of some parallels or analogies, and the simplest one came to mind. When we are asking someone for help or for something, whether this is your employee, your co-worker, or maybe even God! Wouldn't it be easier if you had a relationship? I thought of someone in need of something, let that be YOU. Now would you go out and seek someone you know, or just find the first stranger walking down the street to seek help from?

A lady was calling in to the talk show, talking about how she didn't feel like she was connecting to God when she prayed for stuff. The host made the point, that just as in our human relationships; we need to spend the quality time up front. Get to know Him; just as we need to get to know the employee or co-worker, etc.

He drew the parallel also of the parent and kid, and what if there was no love there; just a kid asking unceasingly for stuff all the time without the loving relationship in place?

Well, I could go on and on here - but I guess you probably see the point. Whether it is about our most important relationship in life, that one with our God, Jesus Christ, or with other humans – nurture the relationship first!

Love songs are different now. This is so cool. In recent years, thanks to Sydney (wife) turning me onto listening to Christian music, an amazing thing has occurred with me. I have started to realize that old favorites, love songs from the past, the really good ones that connect with me, have now taken on a spin they never had previously. Here's the deal: With God now in my life, my number one love in my life, love songs now become about God as the focus vs. some old flame, or just the concept of a significant other. This is very cool. The song not only is still an amazing tune on my old worldly terms, but now it takes on perspectives between God and me, God and others, God and his people that He loves. I just wanted <u>to share that with you.</u>

*A couple of songs that just quickly come to mind that work in this way with me are listed below:

> *When you're down and troubled and you need a helping hand and nothing, whoa, nothing is going right.*
> *Close your eyes and think of me and soon I will be there to brighten up even your darkest nights.*
>
> *You just call out my name, and you know where ever I am I'll come running to see you again.*
> *Winter, spring, summer, or fall, all you have to do is call and I'll be there, yeah, yeah, you've got a friend.*
>
> *If the sky above you should turn dark and full of clouds and that old north wind should begin to blow, keep your head together and call my name out loud.*
> *Soon I will be knocking upon your door.*
> *You just call out my name, and you know where ever I am I'll come running to see you again.*
> *Winter, spring, summer, or fall, all you have to do is call and I'll be there.*
>
> *Hey, ain't it good to know that you've got a friend? People can be so cold.*
> *They'll hurt you and desert you. Well, they'll take your soul if you let them, oh yeah, but don't you let them.*

You just call out my name, and you know where ever I am I'll come running to see you again.
Winter, spring, summer, or fall, all you have to do is call, Lord, I'll be there, yeah, yeah, and you've got a friend.
   You've got a friend.
Ain't it good to know you've got a friend?
Ain't it good to know you've got a friend?
Oh, yeah, yeah, you've got a friend.

A great old song done best by James Taylor and/or Carole King, You've Got A Friend...

And here's another one – Because You Loved Me, performed best by Celine Dion

For all those times you stood by me
For all the truth that you made me see
For all the joy you brought to my life
For all the wrong that you made right
For every dream you made come true
For all the love I found in you
I'll be forever thankful baby
You're the one who held me up
Never let me fall
You're the one who saw me through it all

You were my strength when I was weak
You were my voice when I couldn't speak
You were my eyes when I couldn't see
You saw the best there was in me
Lifted me up when I couldn't reach
You gave me faith 'coz you believed
I'm everything I am
Because you loved me

You gave me wings and made me fly
You touched my hand I could touch the sky
I lost my faith, you gave it back to me
You said no star was out of reach
You stood by me and I stood tall
I had your love I had it all
I'm grateful for each day you gave me
Maybe I don't know that much
But I know this much is true
I was blessed because I was loved by you

You were my strength when I was weak
You were my voice when I couldn't speak
You were my eyes when I couldn't see
You saw the best there was in me
Lifted me up when I couldn't reach
You gave me faith 'coz you believed
I'm everything I am
Because you loved me

You were always there for me
The tender wind that carried me
A light in the dark shining your love into my life
You've been my inspiration
Through the lies you were the truth
My world is a better place because of you

You were my strength when I was weak
You were my voice when I couldn't speak
You were my eyes when I couldn't see
You saw the best there was in me
Lifted me up when I couldn't reach
You gave me faith 'coz you believed
I'm everything I am
Because you loved me

I'm everything I am
Because you loved me

✶✶✶✶✶

My personal relationship with God is one that (just as with people in our lives) gets better and better as we work on it, learn more about HIM, share openly with HIM about ourselves, seek forgiveness, share HIM with others, and for sure, hope to not be judged!

Bottom line? Relationships only improve when we spend time working on them. We can wish and hope things get better with someone, but without doing it, it is just WISHING & HOPING.

Are your relationships good? Are they getting better, fixed, or improved by you doing nothing? Accepting someone as a FRIEND, hoping to have a relationship, or saying someone is your friend is fine; but it only strengthens when we work on it (the relationship).

Just as with GOD, we don't care about someone's world unless we care about the person first.

JUST LOVE EVERYONE, I'LL SORT 'EM OUT LATER

–GOD

The Grit and Grace Project

God is about Relationship, not Religion

It struck me a while back, when it comes to God (as well as with people in our lives): It is not about His Book, it is about the Author!

I have slowly learned that the relationship with our Lord only grows when we first accept HIM, but then that we work to build the relationship. To anyone, God is only a story, a book, or a concept until the personal relationship begins.

Are you spending time quality time with HIM – talking, listening, seeking help, thanking, helping His people, asking forgiveness, understanding, and growing? Do you hang with HIM like you did or do with that best friend?

Again, it is not about His Book, it is about The Author! It is about your relationship with Him. Without it, honestly, the book will be meaningless and useless to you.

The same goes with our human relationships, as mentioned previously,

…People don't care how much you know until they know how much you care.

How about a 'CUP OF COFFEE'…

This is why it is so critical to have a relationship BEFORE you need them, right? Doesn't that make sense? Yet so often people just start functioning around someone, or manage them without focusing on IT until IT is the problem – the undeveloped relationship! I can think of this playing out in so many ways from childhood all the way through becoming an adult.

When do you connect with people; hopefully it is not just when you need something. I see this much in the adult world in many respects, but it begins (and needs to stop if this is you) as younger people, maybe mostly in the teens, and 20's. Somewhere in this range is maybe when it might be the worst – when the young aspiring adult begins to break away from the parent(s) and family. He/she only calls when they need something. If this is still you, break that habit now. There is likely nothing that shows more lack of love than being used which is how those needed without the relationship, do indeed feel. Stay in touch, re-connect, and build the relationship. Have a cup of coffee, even when you don't need anything but their friendship and relationship.

<u>Just a bit more sharing (story I found, cool, huh?)</u>

During my second month of college, our professor gave us a pop quiz. I was a conscientious student and had breezed through the questions until I read the last one:

"What is the first name of the woman who cleans the school?"

Surely this was some kind of joke. I had seen the cleaning woman several times... She was tall, dark-haired and in her 50's, but how would I know her name?

I handed in my paper, leaving the last question empty/blank... Just before class ended, one student asked if the last question would count toward our quiz grade.

"Absolutely", said the professor. "In your careers, you will meet many people. All are significant... They deserve your attention and care, even if all you do is smile and say "hello."

I've never forgotten that lesson. I also learned her name was Dorothy.

LOVE CATEGORIZED

Love has been written about throughout history and with any luck, that trend will never cease because of the importance of the topic. As I think of how love can take on a negative aspect or dysfunction', I quickly go to how I used to think of love. My growth with God, along with my growth in/with my wonderful Sydney (the wife!), has caused me to realize now, way late in life, after the fact, that there are different kinds of love. There is the love one has for God, the one we have for our lover/spouse or significant other, love for child, love for people in general, love for a passion or hobby, etc.

    Before I truly knew God, I used to place the significant other in my life in that role or position. Hang with me here. She would be placed on a pedestal because God was really not yet a relationship in my world. This doesn't work and didn't work. I did not know at the time, but now do know, through learning from my wife and God that HE is that number one relationship. Placing someone else in that lofty position is not only unfair to them, it just won't work. God must be the most important relationship/love in our lives. Everyone else to include that significant other for you is playing second fiddle. I could go on, but will leave you with that to ponder; and sort out for you. Holler if you want to explore it further...

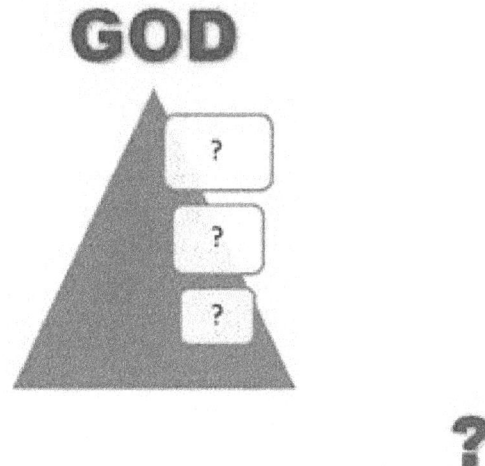

Who or what is competing with or taking the place of God in your worlds of Love & Relationship?

****

Here is how I see the Hierarchy of Love (& Loyalty):

1. It all begins with when we are born (God is there we just don't realize it!)...

2. Initially it is the parents being #1 to the infant (baby)

3. As a child, God should enter the picture and be right there with Mom & Dad...

4. The next level of Godly Love would see God taking the top spot, followed by the parents, siblings, friends, etc.

5. God should always and forever be the #1 spot in terms of your Love

6. Marriage causes a big shift on the worldly level. God should be #1 with both spouses. #2 changes now and the spouse is to now become #2. Children and Parents mesh into #3.

7. God, Spouse, Children, Parents, Siblings, etc.

****

....You do what you wish with all that. I believe that is how it should work; it's important that we in our relationships are on the same page about all this!

DYSFUNCTIONAL **LOVE & RELATIONSHIP** DYNAMICS

Love is such a good thing, I hate to ruin the moment, but feel compelled to mention just a couple of things here.

So many people have been burned by others in some sense, that they have stereotyped the ‗world', and therefore have just lost that loving feeling (as the Righteous Brothers would sing it). There is so much bad in this world, we daily see/read of something so awful that a human being has done to another – it taints our view of mankind and people I believe. Please don't fall into this trap. Love people. I have to believe there are just way more good loving people out there than bad. God directs us to love others. Love people, it will make your world so much more....well significant.

ENABLING: The concept of enabling should be studied and understood by all in leadership roles in this world – parenting, workplace management of people, etc.

Enabling likely feels very much like love to the enabler; having the capacity to see and understand this in our self is, indeed, very difficult. I know this of myself from past experience and for sure see it in others all the time.

This happens within many different kinds of relationships; regardless, the principles involved remain the same. Using the kid and parents relationship, enabling is about that kid you believe you have to do everything for – or else he/she will not make it! Continuing this behavior will prevent them from ever being able to be fruitful in their life, much less be significant. Depending on whether this is YOU, or not, you may not like the rest of this...

Fair is fair however – there will be part(s) of this book that will likely aggravate or upset all of us☺. Some we do well, some we do not. It doesn't change the reality or significance of the principle and how we should practice it (or not).

Enabling might look like: Paying a child's way for everything (such as college maybe) as a parent or grandparent; is that love, enabling, or even crippling to their maturity and growing in a significant way?

This might be about allowing the young adult/your little baby to continue living at home while you repay their college debt, pay for them to live there, listen to their woes, or allow them not to work....all in the name of love. I heard recently on Dave Ramsey's radio show, now that's a Double-triple Whammy and Yikes! Paying for their schooling twice while they live at home – if that ain't enabling, well then...

Maybe you didn't want to hear that huh?

I was so fortunate (in some strange, weird way) to be broke and going through bankruptcy at the time my two kids were ready to go to college. Although I look at them now and see what they accomplished by themselves, I know the parents paying their way concept, can, and is, a bad thing on some level.

I have no real idea what I would have done if I had been able to pay their way through… I just know that they are so capable and responsible today, because they had to learn a whole bunch of things on their own and find their own way to pay, etc. Again that is no pat on my back – I had no option, thank God.

Love and Enabling live on such a fine line – enabling creeps up on the enabler without Him/her, mom/dad, etc. ever realizing what is happening.

Using or taking advantage of others is a close relative to enabling. The enabler or the person being enabled may become a ‚user of others'. It can happen as a subtle outcropping or progression of dysfunctional love dynamics as well. I just know that a healthy, significant, loving relationship doesn't include enabling or using others.

<u>Anyone or anything come to mind at this moment:</u>

…Sooner or later, we must all learn to do it on our own ☺
(Or not) ☹

SIGNIFICANT QUESTIONS ON LOVE & RELATIONSHIP:

1. Do you genuinely like people; just some, very few?

2. Is showing love for others a challenge for you?

3. Who do you let into your networks/relationships?

4. How do you view socializing with people?

5. Is that love or enabling you are being with...?

6. Do people naturally open up to you? [If they know you care, they will...]

7. Do you genuinely enjoy meeting people and spending time with them?

8. What is it that challenges your love for others?

9. Do you see yourself as better than others on some scale?

10. Do you shy away from others or seek to get to know them?

11. Do you stay in touch or expect and hope others will do the work?

12. Has LOVE hurt you and impacted your 'love-significance?

13. Who is the most loving person you know; how about the person you know that seeks to build relations? [What do you think about this person/anything to learn from them?]

14. Do you believe others see you as loveable or...?

15. What is God's teaching(s) to us regarding love and relationships?

FRUITFUL

In a society, workplace and culture where all we tend to focus on is results, money and the bottom line…this should be an easily accepted principle of ours. Fruitfulness is about our actions and results huh? How do we measure the results (fruitfulness) of a person? Is it their number of widgets produced, the size of their house, number of friendships, how well they get it done, their income, etc.? Maybe the principles here (as a whole) should be the measure of the significant person of this world and God's. Love, forgiving, thankfulness, joy, the production and contribution of something to our world…something like that! How are you measured and how do you determine the significance of others? I submit it is somewhere in that 90% that rests below the outward, external and surface of the person that really matters vs. what how things appear on the outside.

Maybe it was Just Seven

As I approach the last of the eight principles, I must tell you that this experience and learning has proven to be anything other than common sense.

For the most part, I am going to ask a whole lot of questions pertaining to Fruitfulness – and how that pertains to Significance.

I discovered recently that biblically some see seven as a symbol of God's completion. I like that concept as it relates to our first seven principles. I think we could have stopped with those seven, but inserted Fruitfulness to be the sum of the first seven. Fruitfulness, to me, seems to be all about the first seven – practicing and leading a walk of the first seven is (BE)-ing fruitful. I am fruitful when my life and walk encapsulates the principles of 1) peace, 2) forgiveness, 3) service, 4) thankful, 5) learning, 6) transparency, 7) love/relationship...

I referenced in the Introduction, how as I pondered these principles in a general sense, they seemed almost logical; too easy, and again, even common sense. As I am now working through this final principle, I can tell you that being principled as described is not simple. It is not easy. In fact, it is work. I think this is the works actually expected of us after accepting God and Jesus.

I am sure you as well, realized the work involved in all this, as you read through the principles - exposing your flaws, sins, shortcomings, and imperfections.

Fruitfulness or being fruitful is last for this reason.

I have to tell you, I also think of being fruitful as using our gifts – whatever those may be. We are gifted with certain God-given skills, talents, capabilities, situations, etc. I believe we are called to use these for the good of all, as well as to build His Kingdom (my God's Kingdom that is). We are fruitful when we produce; when we bear fruit.

What is your fruit?

I believe our fruit can be many different things. It can be in helping others, in productivity, your earnings, your friendships, the numbers you have led to the Lord, etc.

Regardless, there is some production and/or bearing of fruit that should be visible in some way.

In purely human terms, if one does not have a job, does not work, or do some other worthwhile effort here on earth/ in life – can he or she be fruitful? Is it about working and making a living?

I might say the job/work doesn't matter in one sense – if he/she was serving mankind in some other unworldly-accepted way.

That is a stretch, but I am sure it is a gift God could accept if someone never worked a day, but helped people in some way otherwise every day! Here's the deal, as I picture this individual who never got the concept of work or producing anything, does that person have the fruits found in scripture?

The individual who doesn't work, provide for, or make a living financially, is just not going to be THANKFUL. They also will not know PEACE. RELATIONSHIPS & LOVE will be tough on many levels... JOY and KINDNESS toward others will be difficult as this person will have little to no self-esteem. I would guess, he/she would find themselves to be hugely JUDGMENTAL, in defending themselves because they are being judged constantly. Maybe working is a key component to fruitfulness and ultimately significance.

Results, Performance, and Mission Accomplishment are very practical terms which we can all relate to; these concepts are heavily focused on in most workplaces. As we connect the dots regarding fruitfulness, aren't these the fruits expected of us at our jobs? As I think of the workplace here, it makes me think once again, how these principles might just work for a culture's Core Values, Leader, and Employee competencies, etc. What if your workplace or other organizations you are part of, used these principles as their guide and standards for people?

Something interesting has just hit me as I was completing and putting words into this section. If God looks at the lustful heart the same as doing the act of adultery, how does He look at good intentions when it comes to our fruitfulness?

*Do we get credit for thinking about helping someone? I think I know the answer. It is about the heart, mind, and actions taken in everything isn't it?

If my sinful mind tempts me to commit an act, but never follows through with that beautiful woman, how am I graded? If I flirt with that guy, how does that figure in to all this?

In the same sense, again, if all my efforts, good intentions, ideas to help people (being fruitful) all fall short and don't happen - do I get credit?

I am not judging you or anyone here, are you? I must tell you this is all between you and God. I have no certainty or RIGHT answer to these. I will let you ponder that as you move forward in your Significance Journey!

*****

Materialism has been mentioned before, but I will toss it out there again since it has an obvious connection to this principle. One who makes lots of money and buys the best toys, has indeed been successful on some level here on earth. Is that, in itself, significance as well? You know the bumper stickers that say _the guy with the most toys in the end, wins'. Is this right in your mind, or in others you know?

Probably a mind and heart issue again. If my heart is after making lots of money and I take care of my loved ones and help people with it, then it obviously wasn't a bad thing was it?

Joy is not in things but in us.

Robert Wagner

Money is not an easy concept to come to grips with regarding how we are to live – our fruitfulness. I would merely offer up the scripture Lean not on your own Understanding... and then do your best to understand in your heart. We are trying to gain some understanding, and on that note I am going to leave you with a Fruitful-summary of mine...

Fruitfulness is helping others; they are God's loved ones (the people created in His image – the Good, the Bad, and even the Ugly).

Fruitfulness is producing results on this earth that help mankind and are at the same time somehow pleasing to God.

Fruitfulness is growing and making self, others and things better.

Fruitfulness is following God's teachings in terms of loving others, forgiving and being thankful.

Fruitfulness is sowing; reaping rewards is bonus stuff.

<u>*Fruitfulness is doing what is right.*</u>

So please Him in all respects, bearing fruit in every good work. Colossians 1:10

DYSFUNCTIONAL **FRUITFUL** DYNAMICS

When I think of someone who is not FRUITFUL, I think of:

>Someone who sponges off of others and society

>One who uses people for what they can do for him/her

>A person who believes others owe him/her

Someone who has developed the thought, and therefore, in his/her mind, is a victim of....

The unfruitful person now has a victim mentality. I fear this comes from such things as being enabled and/or having taken on crutches in some sense. This is a delicate issue and some won't like this, but I believe we have just become a society that quickly accepts a crutch vs. trying to solve it on our own. I think the crutch-thing is a slippery slope that some get on and cannot break the slide. People have become about drugs, therapy, (booze/smoking probably could fit here as well). I do realize people do need/benefit from drugs and therapy. I just think maybe we jump at these things too quickly anymore, again, beginning that acceptance of forever needing help or a crutch. Clearly, another area where this fits is in the epidemic of ADD and the drugs we so quickly feed kids anymore.

*****

OK, so I made you mad here huh? Well, just consider this, if this isn't you in the dysfunctional sense and you or someone you know has headed down the road of using some crutch because it was really needed – then this isn't about you. If the shoe doesn't fit here, don't wear it☺.

> Someone who has been allowed to remain ungrown and dependent on others (a parent, friend, sibling, etc.)
>
> The enabled individual, given everything
>
> One who does nothing for others?
>
> Everything is about self, him / her problems, issues, etc.
>
> A person with excuses, great intentions, unfulfilled dreams
>
> That person who just talks of going back to school, getting a job, doing this or that, etc....
>
> A person no one wants on his/her team
>
> A person with few friends or significant relationships
>
> Someone with little quality around them in any/all regards
>
> Unproductive, lacking accomplishments
>
> Wouldn't even think of helping someone else
>
> Wouldn't normally think of others in any sense, other than how others might help their world
>
> Broke financially, in spirit, and in relationships

Anyone or anything come to mind at this moment:

Pessimist - one who uses tomorrow's clouds to block today's sunshine?

SIGNIFICANT QUESTIONS ON FRUITFUL:

1. How do you visualize someone that is fruitful?

2. What do you consider to be your fruits?

3. Is anyone proud of you for something(s) other than just for existing and consuming oxygen?

4. As you think about the fruit on the vine analogy (or scripture), what comes to mind for you in thinking about people?

5. Take a look back at the previous 7 principles in this book. How do you view them as pertaining to being fruitful?

6. Is someone enabling you, thus keeping you from being fruitful; are you enabling someone doing the same?

7. Can you think of someone(s) in your life that is not bearing fruit? What is preventing them from doing so? Could you help them?

8. How can you become more ‗bearing of fruit'?

9. Are you someone who makes things happen and is highly productive in your daily walk at work, etc.?

10. How do you think others see you in relationship to the fruits described in scripture (love, joy, peace, patience, kindness, goodness, faithfulness, gentleness and self-control, ...)

11. When was the last time you saw / experienced someone demonstrating their ‚fruitfulness'?

12. How do the concepts of potential and intention relate to fruitfulness?

13. Do you have a resume of accomplishments, learning, results, and achievements?

14. Do you believe others see you as being fruitful on this earth?

15. How do you think God sees your fruitfulness?

WRAPPING UP .... The Principles!

> My to-do list for today:
>
> - Count my blessings
> - Practice kindness
> - Let go of what I can't control
> - Listen to my heart
> - Be productive yet calm
> - Just breathe

IN CONCLUSION - As promised earlier; here is the question I said I would ask of you at our conclusion:

Do you see how adapting and adopting these principles in your life will lead to peace, happiness and significance?

As I put a wrap on this book and do that *conclusion thing*; I will ask you to go first.

> What are your thoughts right now in moving forward in your life? In a few sentences, what is on your mind in summarizing a few key take-away(s) for you right now?

...Do you realize in a year from now you might be wishing you had started now?

There is a cool thing about this -starting now- deal. As we work on ourselves, we are granted a grace-period; that is God's Grace. Maybe we should think of this as a DO-OVER.

Regardless, we better be diligently working on significance as we never know when we need to be there - when our work needs to be finished. Of course this is just to say that He will come again and we had better be walking a significant walk with Him. If you are not a Believer, but die tonight, how will you be remembered? Are there things needing fixing, anything undone?

I discovered an interesting parallel between my work and passions in contrast to our significance principles walk:

1. LEADERSHIP DEVELOPMENT
2. FAITH
3. SIGNIFICANCE (these principles, changing behaviors, etc.)

Many folks believe the application of these concepts to be an issue of time. I have heard for many years from managers viewing leadership practices as something they must find an extra hour in the day to do! After they do their real work and after the day is done - they will tack on some extra time to walk around and be nice to people!

I think there are parents that think of parenting in that same way; if I just tack on an extra hour periodically that will make me be a good parent.

I hear the same about God. It is as if it is about scanning your planner/calendar to find an extra 10 minutes to read the bible, say a prayer and spend some extra time about Him.

These are all well intended good starts, but in all three cases our significance goal is to walk that walk all day long.

1. LEADERSHIP DEVELOPMENT: Taking care of people, teaching, helping, relating and supporting as I manage this place.
2. PARENTING: Teaching, caring for, listening, relating and being there for the kids throughout their days.
3. FAITH: Carrying on a dialogue with Him. Building the relationship; doing His work in our relationships and having conversation all day, every day, and every minute. As if He were there with you everywhere (cuz He is ☺).
4.

This is all about living these principles in all of our Walks of Life. The challenge in these roles is to internalize and make them BE-come your walk in your daily life. The principles and practices here are who we need to become, who we are! It is not about plugging into your planner: time to lead, parent or do the God thing! Of course these are challenging, but are our goal right? Again you and I will never be perfect. I believe that is okay. Remember, it is the journey.

The challenge here is, on a personal level, how will you daily improve in these significance principles? On a bigger picture, who might need some of your counsel, mentoring and teaching about these principles and improving their life? By the way, teaching about them is a great way to grow and improve you.

What is my purpose, what have I done, what could I still do, what do I want to have as my legacy? What will I be remembered for? I hope you have by now begun to really work on these. I also hope you will pass them on either through your modeling or teaching to others – to include your future generations (your children and beyond).

So what will be your legacy or is it still undecided (of course it is not lived out, but you could decide about your path? Will it be about past stuff screwed up, or stuff still to happen? We may have one day left or many years left, what is yet to be done? So maybe this is the main point here (you were hoping I would get to it huh?):

Actually we mentioned this earlier and you have heard it before; we all know it to be true...

It won't be about material STUFF, but will be about others - relationships, and those we have HELP-ed, FORGIVE-n, LOVE-d...and those we have <u>NOT helped, forgiven or loved</u>!

Maybe you are still pretty young?! Why wait to get focused on the Right Stuff? Remember all those others around us are God's children, just like we are.

Chasing the dream – for me I am trying now, these days, to do what I believe is God's purpose for me ...helping others. I truly believe focusing and practicing these...

> PEACE
> FORGIVE
> SERVE
> LEARN
> TRANSPARENCY
> THANK
> LOVE
> FRUITFULNESS

....will cause us to achieve significance (along with that belief thing in God, and Jesus Christ.

Have an amazingly significant day!

Booker

(I owe it to you to share this): MY FAITH, MY GOD

One of my purposes with this book was to be transparent in every sense. In doing so, I absolutely want to share with you (and more specifically a few very important people in my life), my beliefs about God and our Salvation. This is truly one of the aspects of this book that made it something I had to do; and pretty much rushed to get done! Maybe it will provide a way for you to share your faith with others in your worlds, through this book and specifically this that follows....

For those I love so dear and who may not know precisely where I am coming from, here is what I believe. I know there are many in my life and within my worlds (blogs, e-Blasts, books, etc.) who see me saying stuff that isn't who they knew me as (from our previous relationship and previous seasons of mine). I am the same, just different my friend. I still am the same character you knew me as in many ways with flaws, practices, imperfections, etc. that don't seem to fit in with God talk. Well, read on - but again I am different, but still the same☺.

It is my hope that this book will provide a starting point for dialogue between us. By the way, this invitation is there for anyone reading this who feels compelled. Even if we do not really know each other at this very moment, I hope that will change. For now let's be transparent –I will go first!

I grew up in church with loving parents who had me there every Sunday. Many times this involved making me get out of bed, being dragged there sleepy-eyed and for sure riding there unwillingly. I heard concepts, stories, preaching's and scriptures about God, a Holy Ghost, God's son Jesus who supposedly died on a cross and came back alive a few days later. This is who we referenced as God, the trinity - who we pray to; ask stuff of, say grace to, before eating, etc.

As I sit here closing in on 60 years of experiences behind me, I am unsure what I really thought or believed about the reality of all that back then.

I suppose I considered myself a Christian, but fairly sure I knew nothing of being what I now know of being a Believer. I knew nothing really about being saved, being born again and other now-familiar concepts.

I loved lots of church things as well. We had a cool pastor for several years during my teen years who took us out socializing, befriended us and things like that. Church camp in the Ozarks area during four summers was very awesome – I still think of the songs -Swing Low Sweet Chariot, Kumbaya and a cute little girl I thought I was in love with (more to that story but you'll have to wait for another time to hear it).

Skipping way ahead, I was 50 years old when life changed through crisis in my life. I was divorcing, going through bankruptcy, making decisions that nearly caused me to lose my kids, lost respect of other loved ones - when the Lord led a humble preacher into my path. He helped me through that period while also facilitating my understanding of what a Christian really was. I will always owe him, Ronnie Black my life.

To make a long story a bit shorter, In the middle of one of our learning times together, I realized what I had missed previously. Here's the deal for me anyway; for those much more capable of conveying this message than I - forgive any incorrectness in how I communicate this. It's my way of thinking of it all. It's what's in my mind and heart.

!!! This saved or being born again thing is all about understanding and accepting (believing REALLY) that there was a Jesus who REALLY was God's son; who REALLY did come down to live here on earth and who did die on a cross for us. He REALLY did rise and come back to life about three days later; and soon thereafter returned back to heaven REALLY. He will REALLY come again when this world, as we know it comes to an end. I also believe that all of those who get this and accept it along with his forgiveness will be taken up to Heaven to live eternally with our God, Jesus and the Holy Spirit.

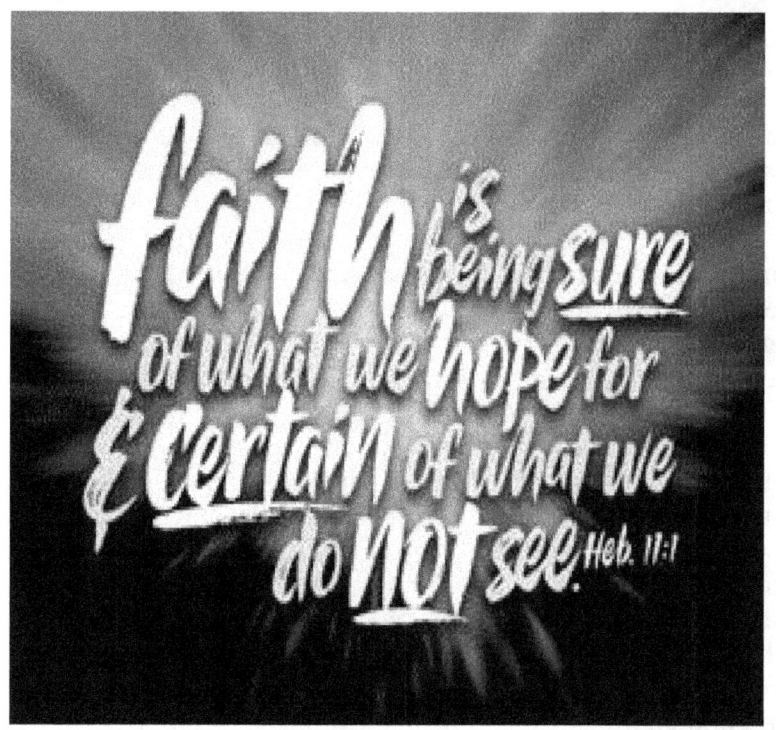

There you have it, my belief. There is no in between.

Those who denied God here in this world, and did not believe will go to another place a whole lot less desirable. This was another reason for my urgency in getting this book completed...

Now there are many dynamics of all this that I will not attempt to get into here right now. Not only because I want to keep this short, but also because there is much I do not understand about all the details, and how all of this happens and plays out... Most of the rest is just God's ways and how it all occurs; the Why's & How's of God's ways. I will say that most of the rest of anything you may hear is to me about denomination, man-made rules, religion, etc. However that is the essence of what my belief and what real faith is about, my asking God to forgive my sins and to be accepted into His Kingdom.

After accepting this, I can walk the walk of God's teachings. As a whole, that's what the bible is, our set of instructions. When one accepts Jesus as their Lord and

Savior, they are beginning anew and they now have a *growing* personal relationship with God through his son Jesus. The person is then saved or born again as we hear it phrased. This newness of who we are is maybe where these significance principles kick in and need to become our walk from there forward.

For me, I love that relationship with Jesus; who I communicate with in my mind and heart nearly most moments of every day (now).

We are sinners; we are all flawed and imperfect. Sins are forgiven if we are, in our heart, truly sorrowful and seek His forgiveness. When we continue to sin deliberately believing that it is not of concern, because He will forgive us – we are wrong I believe. We likely are not truly saved and were not really born again if that is the thinking. All this is about the Mind and the Heart. This is dealing with this whole issue of sin and forgiveness with the mind only. When we add the heart to the mix and we are truly trying to stop sinning, now we can be forgiven and significance can be achieved. We are born again, saved and however you want to say it.

I believe that anyone and everyone are welcome to become part of His Kingdom and to His amazing grace. He (God) is merciful and will accept anyone who is willing and will try to follow His commandments as laid out in the bible, his Word.

As we spoke to in the intermission of this book, He answers our prayers and cares for us. However He does things in His own way.
Much of that will never be understood by us.

As mentioned earlier, I have become okay with that thought process; it makes sense I should not understand God's ways. He is God and I am an ant...!

So with that in mind, let me again say it is my belief that once we have begun this journey with God and Jesus His Son, we are to attempt to walk His walk. I am expected to grow this relationship by growing me (myself) - which is where these eight (8) principles fit in for me. My attempt was to extract what I believe to be the essence of what we are supposed to be like, in following His model.

Let me briefly tell you what I do not believe faith and my God are about, Before you read on, please know I am not suggesting any of these are good or bad practices / concepts. They can be distracters and are just not at the core of what my faith and belief is about:

> Church buildings
> Denomination
> Places where perfect people congregate
> Singing, dancing, waving arms in the air How one dresses
> Judging
> Kneeling, standing or sitting
> Water over one's head
> Communion
> Religion
> And in general, man-made rules guessing how we are to practice God…

These are areas where God gets a bad rap from some outsiders trying to find Him. I read from a book by Francis Schaeffer put it into a perspective I like. He said essentially that our faith in God is not anything mechanical. It is nothing to do with IF you do this, IF you do it that way, IF …anything. It is not HOW one does it in their church, denomination or religion. It is simply … (simply could be a stretch, as there is nothing simple about God and how He does his work☺) …about confessing our sins, accepting Jesus and the personal ongoing relationship with Him.

One tip to share here with anyone, Christian, Believer or not: If you do not have a personal relationship with Jesus – then His book, the bible, His Word will mean little. It is about the author, not the book. The bible never worked for me until I knew Him.

Just as in communication issues and barriers we may have with someone on this earth; it is not about the message but rather it is about the sender (or the

_receiver'). Regardless how you put it or say it, if the relationship isn't there, communication and the message(s) will be unclear. I will let you chew on that further on your own...

These (8) principles are at least a great start to how we should walk our daily walk; of that I am sure. These combined with an ever-developing relationship with Him will (for me as I understand it) lead to an eternal life in His Kingdom. Having mastered the principles will not have just made me and you significant in this world, but significant in His eyes. Living a solid relationship with Jesus will make us worthy of existing in His Eternal World. That's all I got for now.

...It doesn't and won't get any better than that when that day comes.

Before finishing this section, let me offer to you a prayer to offer to God if you at this moment would want all this I just described. If you choose this (or not for that matter), I would love to hear from you, to pursue a relationship and help each other grow beyond this moment☺. This is the essence of what it is all about and a prayer to Him:

ALMIGHTY GOD, I come to you through your Son Jesus. I wish to be part of your Kingdom and forgive me of my sins, flaws and imperfections. I need you in my life.
I know now that you Jesus died on a cross for me and all of us. I believe this in all my heart and mind that you God raised your son Jesus from the dead.
I accept Jesus as my Savior and my friend. I want a lasting relationship to

help me through nature of sin, to walk a walk that would be pleasing to you God.

Thank you Jesus for your Grace and mercy in forgiving me and all my many mistakes and bad choices in life.

Thank you for accepting me as one of yours and saving me – giving me eternal life.

Thank you for transforming my life; help me to learn and grow according to your Will and your Word. I love you Jesus and thank you for all the blessings in my life.

[….now you add anything else, you may wish to, below]

Amen.

PIECES OF SIGNIFICANCE

> This section is intended to be a whole bunch of......key, practical, applicable lessons and best practices for life. Some information is restating and simplifying what was said somewhere earlier. Some content is reinforcement of what was presented over the previous few hundred pages. Much of it is scripturally based, from the heart, from God. Some just me.
>
> There is plenty here that is just my advice, suggestion and thinking regarding life; what I have learned as good stuff to do in life. Some just didn't quite fit elsewhere however I wanted it included.
>
> These are in no particular order, just all good stuff I am sure you will agree!

So, here we go...

There are plenty of times in life and conversations where we really don't know what we are talking about, seriously. Some that we are just plain wrong about as well. Some of these areas might be politics, religion, other's experiences with experiences we haven't had, someone else's challenges, etc. >Significant people recognize when they are just talking opinions & assumption-stuff and learn to SHUT UP, LISTEN or ASK QUESTIONS.

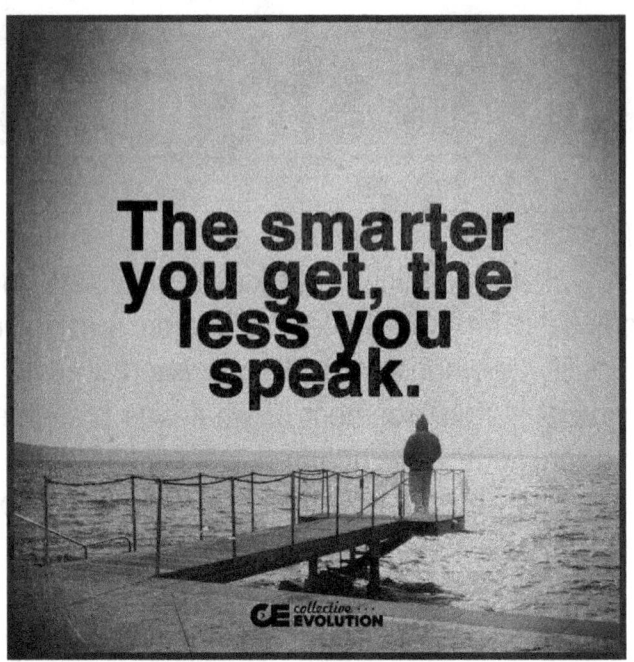

Early on, FIND Dave Ramsey (radio/podcasts), or some other individual who can coach and teach you how to do your life financially. How to not be broke, how to not suffer through bankruptcy at some point, how to stay out of debt and take care of you for life, financially speaking.

> If you are after these principles, you need to take care of this or you are liable to end up insignificant in regard to a few of these principles: being UNFRUITFUL, incapable of SERVICE (giving to others), etc. This is just another one of those important parts of life many of us were never taught, and therefore just believed it would all work out. Well it won't without a plan and some strategy for living significantly. You get it, right?

Do not live a life stereotyping others. What one did to you, the rest of the world didn't do! What one did for you, the rest of the world won't necessarily. Everyone is different, no one is the same. Do not assume one of us is like the other. Don't stop trusting because you were betrayed by one (or more) on this earth. You get it right?

Take care of yourself physically. Find something during every season of life that you can do to stay at least minimally fit. It has to be something you can enjoy and will do because you know how good it makes you feel, the stress it relieves, etc. Just like your finances, this does not just happen naturally.

Leave notes for people. My dad tore a piece of paper from something and left me a note after a big high school football game saying how proud he was of me. I still have that note. My wife leaves me little notes on the bathroom mirror frequently. These are such simple little things to do – a great practice to get into...

Do unto others as you would want God to be unto you.

Say you are SORRY quickly; own up to your failures/mistakes. You will make them because you are not perfect. Trying to fool people into believing you are (perfect and incapable of mistakes) is freaking crazy thinking.

Very likely saying you understand isn't the best thing to say at times - although well intentioned. Choose something else unless you really have walked in those shoes and do understand.

Wave, greet folks and say hello before they do. Initiate kindness. Initiate possible friendships or recognize daily people in your life. Whatever you do - don't look down/away. Why do people do that?

Build on and strengthen current relationships constantly. Keep them alive, all of them even if they do not help. Seek to add new people in your life routinely. You never know the significance of anyone for you, to you, that you might be able to help, etc. New people add to our growing and LEARNING. A new person may just be a personality in which you need to discover and learn to work.

Fix damaged relationships immediately (that goes for you leaders out there with your teams, your peers and your boss). If they are not cooperative, fix it anyway. It is insane to leave yourself in conflict with others in your world(s). Even if this means, you have to let them believe they won something, let them win. By letting them win, you will also win insanity out of your life.

Don't do anything you don't want to be transparent about; stuff you don't want said about you or yelled in the hallways at school or church. BTW (that's computer talk for by the way BTW☺)... Facebook is a great way for people to find out about you. It is funny how people won't be transparent in person but will publish for the world on Facebook stuff they really don't want some people to read or think about themselves. That company you are interviewing for will go there first to find out who you really are – what will they see?

Balance is important. My life's experiences bring me to a point of believing this concept you and I have likely heard somewhere. Too much of anything is a bad thing... Anything in moderation... Anything and everything you have a choice about should be done or pursued in balance with the other significant aspects of your life. I am fairly sure that too much of anything is indeed in some way going to lead to some re-balancing you may not like.

> This all goes from a diet and what you eat/drink, to the principles talked to here. Even too much of any one principle here may leave another area lacking which maybe leaves you overall insignificant. I am sure that is true now as I think about it; what do you think? Now put down that package of cookies and go get a carrot☺.

Be THANKFUL before you receive; that attitude likely will result in you finally actually getting it. I have a friend, J.L -. that typifies this significance better than anyone I have ever met.
> He has so many struggles and troubles in his life. He possesses so little, but is likely the most THANKFUL person I know on this earth. Thank you J.L. for being such a great example of this to all those around you – including me for sure.

Find your Transparency Line with all people. Go for it, it is where anything/everything good between you can and will happen.

We all know and realize how wealth and materialism can be the destruction of man. Be careful with this if you become successful in this regard - Possessing wealth is not wrong, but wealth possessing you is'. I believe this happens easily.

...it is easier for a camel to go through the eye of a needle than for a rich man to enter the kingdom of God. Matthew 19:24

Most of us having experienced some amount of life already have come to realize that many things could have turned out better if we had just been where we should have been' at that moment.

Help someone today; if you make their day better, so will yours be.

Open doors for others. Let them enter the elevator first. Think of them first...

"Life's most persistent and urgent question is: **'What are you doing for others?'**" - Dr. Martin Luther King, Jr.

It is our nature that we are all anything BUT open-minded regarding how things should be, should be done, etc. Are you a perfectionist and have to have things done YOUR way? BTW, if you are this way and you are in a leadership role - this is a REAL problem.

If you ask someone how they are doing - stop and really listen. If you don't care, why ask; it will be taken as a totally insincere question you realize? If they ask you, tell them (after asking if they really want to know).

Life is indeed not fair seemingly at times. Lean not on your own Understanding -says our God. It is at those times when we should give thanks. It works. Chew on that one for a moment.

Don't let the negative interactions with one person in life turn you against the rest of the people in the world. You know that person (friend, family or foe) that lied and betrayed you; that was him/her - not everyone else. Do not let that one person make you into a distrusting individual who won't let others in your life. Most people are good – you heard it here first.

If you struggle with losing, with being wrong or not being right, you are wrong – get past it! LEARN to be okay with being wrong, looking stupid, etc. We all cannot know everything or always be right. Besides BE-ing HUMBLE is a good thing.

People will tell you - Just pray and He will take care of it. Sometimes yes. However it is not that simple; you may be praying for something that you will discover down the road wasn't in your best interest. When that happens give thanks that He didn't answer that prayer, right? Yes, pray and He will answer it in His own way on His own schedule. Ever been glad He didn't answer some prayer of yours?

If you are a young adult at the beginning stages of life, know this: You don't know what you don't know. Seek wisdom by listening to those who have been where you are... It doesn't mean they are smarter than you, just older and know more about some stuff. The significant person listens and learns from others who have been down your road. They aren't just old, they know stuff.

Forgive frequently and quickly; anyone you are holding a grudge against at this moment?

Treat God, and more directly His Son Jesus as your best friend. What makes a best friend your best friend? I'm betting it is all pretty closely related to the practice of eight principles. How we practice these principles with God is tied to how effectively we will practice them here with others.

I believe God answers all prayers with YES, NO or WAIT. Yes - is what we want to hear, No - we do not want to hear. Wait - maybe is the worse one to deal with for any of us.

Realize that your common-sense is not others; what is obvious to you is not necessarily obvious to everyone else. Trust the coach on this, not understanding this dynamic is one of the biggest struggles for people in working with others, teamwork, decision-making, work success, etc.

Others are not necessarily going to see things the way you do – in many cases this is a good thing. This does not mean they are the enemy. Difference is not a bad thing unless unresolved. And in regards to all this: vice versa

Focus on others. It will keep you happy and out of sorrow, depression and self-pity. When you are wallowing in your own sorrows, throw your focus on others, it will serve you well.

Find Accountability Partners in your life to help you with the practice of these Principles of Significance

---

Routinely thank everyone who help you in your world ...and thank God all day long.

That person behind the counter (serving/helping you or otherwise having to deal with you) did not make it 102-dang degrees today. They did not cause your emergency or make you miserable. Don't take it out on them. They have their own stuff to deal with and have no reason to be blamed for yours.

There is one in every crowd - you know what I mean? If you do not know what I mean or don't see one in every crowd...well you might just be the one. You know what I mean?

Do not loan or accept loans from friends or loved ones. I'm just sayin'...

Realize being wrong and admitting it, makes you human. Not realizing or admitting makes you a jerk.

The challenge of diversity these days is really not so much about race, gender and other physical differences. The challenge for all of us is just working with, functioning or existing with people who think differently than we do. How they do stuff, how they logic, how they reason, where they put their trash can, how they chew their gum, etc. Also please realize we are all an –other- to others! Fix the relationship with those others in your life. You do realize you are an -other- to others, don't you? Any insanity relationships in your world needing fixing – not living that Groundhog Day movie are you?

People over stuff always - including money and the pursuit of it.

Dreams are an awesome thing to have and work toward. Make sure you are walking toward them in a significant way. It is once again about the journey.

When you are doing God's work (good stuff), the devil will be after you. When you are away from God, Satan will likely just let you aimlessly stumble along and do the stupid stuff you are now doing. I'm just saying!

Place God as your #1 above anything, everything or anyone in your life.

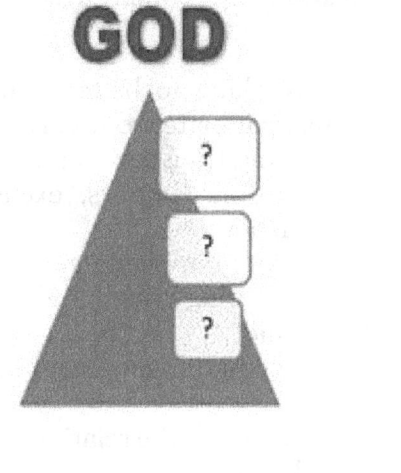

Everyone and Everything else is a distant #2. People (or anything you put in a box here) will let you down in some respect, disappoint, and/or will fail you eventually. If you keep Him in this position, He will always be there. He will be there regardless even if you haven't spotted Him.

> *IF this intrigues you, let me send you my LITTLE GOD BOOK as I call it. Actually it is titled: 'Triangles, Compasses & GOD'. Happy to send you FREE eBook!

Realize all others around us are just flawed imperfect folks like you; most are just doing their best just like you. Some are not and need your significance.

Ponder, understand, study the meaning and live this quote: **"People don't care how much you know until first they know how much you care."** It is relevant to your life, believe me.

Any Significant Relationship is one worth:

...Working to better understand him/her & make it better routinely
...Being transparent and open with them
...Finding time vs. excuses, to spend with him/her
...Giving forgiveness
...Listening first and getting listened to secondly
...Unconditional acceptance and no judging

...You place the relationship first; petty stuff is a distant second
...Have a cup of coffee (and coffee is not the point here) with someone before you need them. Do it before a conflict arises or some other difference challenges you two – because it will.

...You remain in peace; conflicts/differences get resolved quickly
...You help, give & support him/her
...You share perspectives & honest opinion to help each other improve
...Being open minded; welcoming critique & can live with being wrong
...You learn & grow from them and vice versa
...You appreciate him/her
...We become better because of it (the relationship); better in our lives - work & play

Tell those people who mean something to you that they mean something to you - before it's too late. Let them know you love them before something happens. Listen to the old folks about this one, they know.

Carry around a business card(s) always. Get this done and don't procrastinate or stew about what it should say; improve on it later. Get it done, with your basic contact information. You never know when you will cross paths with someone you hope to see/meet again and have no pencil/paper. How many times has this happened in your life already?

GIVING is long term stuff; RECEIVING is totally short term stuff.

Never Stop Learning in all of your worlds – work, play, relationships. It is true that if things are not changing, you are not growing. When you stop insignificant.

Nearly everyone else around you is also dealing with some very stressful problem, issue or challenge.

What you sow is in direct relationship with what you will reap. What you plant is what you will harvest. No seed, no growth. Plant good seeds. These all possibly connect with what goes around/comes around'...

Insignificant people will try to tear you down in life. Are you really going to allow something/someone so insignificant to do that to you? Never give someone permission to tear you down. They can't if you don't.

Accept gifts given to you. Do not prevent someone from receiving the blessing that comes from _giving'. Take it, accept it and say thank you.

Foul language, don't use it. What you say is who you are. Some say it just demonstrates how limited your vocabulary is? If it is a habit, break it - one of these days you will pay for it in some regard. Also remember, you are ALWAYS marketing yourself. Trust the coach on this...

Smile and make others smile; if smiling is new to your face, you will love what happens. Watch how people will be so puzzled and wonder what's up! That will lead to good things.

"WHEN YOU REALLY PAY ATTENTION EVERYTHING IS YOUR TEACHER."

Unknown

> For you (the eBook or KINDLE Reader), find some paper/pencil and truly work on this...

SELF-ASSESSMENT

I want to encourage you to take a breath, find some free time and then take this assessment. The intent here is for you to review your thinking, reflections, concerns, issues, intentions and actions considered from each of the eight principles.

Within each principle you learned something new or were reminded of something you had forgotten. What comes to mind of significance right now? Just try to capture some general thoughts here, what do you remember; what impacted you about you? Go back within reading on each principle and review comments you made....

PEACE

FORGIVING

SERVICE

LEARNING

TRANSPARENCY

THANKFUL

LOVE/RELATIONSHIP

FRUITFUL

> *You were challenged to assess yourself at the end of each principle / section. Re-assess yourself now.

Principle:　　　　　　　　　　　1: Low / 10: High

PEACE　　　　　　　　　　　_____

FORGIVING　　　　　　　　　_____

SERVICE　　　　　　　　　　_____

LEARNING　　　　　　　　　_____

TRANSPARENCY　　　　　　　_____

THANKFUL　　　　　　　　　_____

LOVE/RELATIONSHIP　　　　　_____

FRUITFUL　　　　　　　　　　_____

*What is your action plan for improving? Who will help you get there? How committed are you to improving? What's your timeline to achieving levels of improvement? How will you know you have improved?

PEACE

FORGIVING

SERVICE

LEARNING

TRANSPARENCY

THANKFUL

LOVE/RELATIONSHIP

FRUITFUL

Lastly, if any sustainable change is hoped for here, how will you prevent this from becoming just a nice read, some good stuff to consider, or this book as well as your thoughts just to set on a shelf gathering dust?

Date(s) to Revisit? (Place on your calendar!?!

EPITAPH
(or Mission Statement)

We began the book asking how you saw your significance; how you wanted to be viewed when your time comes and how you wanted to be remembered. In the spirit of the asking and your now having read this, what better way to determine and define your mission in life than to write your epitaph now?

Here's my thought: What you want your epitaph (and/or obituary) to read just might clarify your Life's Mission Statement. This can always change but it is a good way to place your intent here right now. Maybe after getting it to read the way you like, maybe it would be a good thing to keep on your wall, close at hand, somewhere...

My Epitaph & Life's Mission Statement
(Where you are going from here ...significantly):

AUTHOR

Doug and his significant-other, Sydney currently reside in Woodstock, GA. Sydney helps people; leads others to the Lord and works with Hospice (care taking) – and puts up with husband Doug. Doug works with helping individuals and organizations grow – in their Leadership, Faith and Relationships... personally and/or professionally. Nearly 15 years a Military Army Infantry Officer and 25 years now in Leadership and OD work. About a dozen years now with God fully aboard!

www.bookertraining.com / 913.232.0244

Linked In, Facebook, Twitter or email: doug@bookertraining.com

> "...Life can only be understood backwards. Unfortunately it must be lived forward." — Kierkegaard

...SIGNIFICANCE, to me, is about the moment and how we live it. I believe God wants us focused at this time, right now – this very moment. He wants us to seek forgiveness and forget the past; and not to worry about the future.

My prayer for you and I is that we can continue to grow in how we live, and learn in Him and His Way(s).

Regarding the knuckleheads and others on this earth (you, me, all of us) - I pray we can find peace and achieve productive connectivity. I pray that you and I will meet and BE - in some significant way.

I pray that we will always focus on serving others; BE thankful for even the little things; and transparently achieve love in our relationships.

By placing God in first place and every moment practicing these principles, we will BE fruitful.

I pray we will all find significance in this life, starting now - finishing strong and well. *In His Name, Jesus!*

Significance

We're done here, however... Let's

...NEVER STOP LEARNING, and GROWING!

READER NOTES....

READER NOTES....

READER NOTES....

READER NOTES....

www.ingramcontent.com/pod-product-compliance
Lightning Source LLC
Chambersburg PA
CBHW060150050426
42446CB00013B/2761